DANCE INJURIES

DANCE INJURIES
their prevention and care

Daniel D. Arnheim

Professor, California State University,
Long Beach

with

Joan Schlaich

Associate Professor, Dance Department,
School of Fine Arts, California State University,
Long Beach

with 125 *illustrations; drawings by* **Helene Arnheim**

The C. V. Mosby Company

Saint Louis   1975

Library of Congress Cataloging in Publication Data

Arnheim, Daniel D
    Dance injuries, their prevention and care.

    Bibliography: p.
    Includes index.
    1. Dancing—Accidents and injuries. I. Schlaich,
Joan, joint author. II. Title. [DNLM: 1. Dancing.
2. Sport medicine. 3. Wounds and injuries—Prevention
and control. 4. Wounds and injuries—Therapy.
WA487.D4 A748d]
GV1595.A73   613.7   74-22491
ISBN 0-8016-0313-7

E/M/M 9 8 7 6 5 4 3 2

Foreword

This is the first book about the care and prevention of injuries to concern itself exclusively with dance and dancers.

Dr. Arnheim is uniquely qualified to write this book. He has a rare combination of experiences: kinesiologist, former athletic trainer, and currently a teacher for the Long Beach Summer School of Dance on the Prevention and Care of Dance Injuries. He has also been "on call" for care of injuries to all 225 students of the summer school for the past seven years.

We found that students who were in his classes were teaching other students at the summer school how to tape their injuries, care for their calluses, and eat properly (instead of the typical unsound fad diets we see with our students), as well as how to warm up safely. The students in the Long Beach regular academic year dance program also consult Dr. Arnheim about their conditioning problems.

Dr. Arnheim is greatly concerned about dancers and the care of their bodies. He has seen many unnecessary injuries and is concerned that dancers understand their bodies better and protect them more sensibly. This book has grown out of the knowledge he has gained in his work with dancers and with the kinds of injuries that are prevalent among students and professionals.

This book is designed to be used as a text for a course in kinesiology and prevention and care of dance injuries. In fact, this is the kind of book every dancer should have on hand. When an injury occurs, it is an immediate source of advice—what to do now and what to continue doing as you go on dancing despite an injury (as dancers usually do).

Our thanks go to our students who posed for the photographs, often in uncomfortable or injury-fraught poses, in order to show "how not to"—Gwen Henry, Margaret Ezekial, and Bob Dulaney, as well as those in Dr. Arnheim's Summer School of Dance class.

Joan Schlaich

Preface

Dance Injuries: Their Prevention and Care is a practical guide to be used by the professional and amateur dancer as well as the teacher, the student, and the choreographer. The most up-to-date information is afforded the reader on prevention and management of dance injuries, both acute and chronic. Technical terms are kept to a minimum, but when required they are clearly defined in the glossary.

It is imperative that individuals in the dance profession thoroughly understand the best means of preventing and caring for the most common dance injuries. Dance teachers also must know when injuries are beyond the scope of their particular background and require the assistance of a specialist. Many performance hours and days as well as entire careers may be saved by following the proper methods of injury prevention and care. Also, teachers of dance must understand the limits of the human body and be able to impart the best injury preventive methods available to their students. They should be able to counsel students on the best means of managing dance injuries. It is hoped that this guide will eliminate much of the fadism, old wives' tales, and superstitions about the care of the body that are currently so characteristic of the dance profession.

The book is divided into five basic parts. Part 1, The Focus, introduces the reader to the field of traumatic medicine. It also indicates historical and current influences on the prevention and care of injuries due to physical activity. Part 2, The Causes of Dance Injury, discusses the ramifications of how injuries are incurred by the dancer. Body structure and posture are discussed in depth, as well as the use and misuse of the body in dance. Part 3, Injury Prevention, discusses conditioning, warm-up, nutrition, and psychological factors inherent in the dance profession. Part 4, Principles of Injury Care, gives the bases for evaluating and providing therapy for the dance injury. Cold and heat therapy are discussed in depth, along with massage and reconditioning exercises. The principles of using protective and supportive materials are also discussed. Part 5, Common Dance Conditions, utilizes the information that has been imparted in earlier chapters to thoroughly understand the most prevalent injuries occurring to the dancer. Chapters in this section are dedicated to the discussion of compression injuries, including contusions, friction problems, strains, and joint and skeletal problems consisting of sprains, dislocations, and fractures. Under each of these injury categories, management is discussed in detail along with the important supportive and protective techniques that can be applied to the body by the dancer.

To further assist the reader in understanding the material, numerous photographs, drawings, and charts are presented throughout. Where practical, methods of taping or wrapping are indicated; step-by-step instructions with specific illustrations are also provided.

I am grateful for the many helpful suggestions that have been put forth by both teachers and students. Without their interest and stimulation, this book would have been an impossible project. A special thanks is extended to Helene Arnheim for her help with the manuscript and illustrations.

Daniel D. Arnheim

Contents

part five   Common dance conditions

DANCE INJURIES

Dancers must be able to apply scientific principles to the prevention and care of injuries. Dr. Arnheim and Long Beach Summer School of Dance students in his class "The Prevention and Care of Dance Injuries."

part one

_____

The focus

Because dancers place great and unusual demands on their bodies, there is a need for special attention to the prevention of injury and the ability to properly care for the body when an injury occurs. Dancers must be able to apply scientific principles of training in order to physically and emotionally withstand the innumerable stresses imposed by this art form. They must also be aware of when injuries are beyond the scope of their knowledge and experience and must know the key signs that indicate that a physician is needed. To these ends *Dance Injuries: Their Prevention and Care* is dedicated.

chapter one

Introduction

Dance is an art form in which the body is the instrument of expression. In seeking maximum expression of style and technique, dancers often exceed their capacities. The result is an injury that may be temporary or, in many cases, permanent. This may possibly exclude the dancer from all future participation in dance. In seeking optimum response from the body and mind, the dancer may exceed the physiological limitations of the body. Lack of knowledge of these limitations and understanding of when rest is needed or when a particular therapy might be beneficial often causes the dancer needless inactive time and incapacitation.

There is no physical endeavor that can be compared to dance when seeking perfection of movement. Few sports can compare with dance in terms of time, energy, and physical demands placed on the mind, body, and spirit (Fig. 1-1).

In contrast to dance, athletics in the United States has the know-how to prevent and properly care for the traumatic injuries that can occur in particular sports. It is obvious that the athlete in the United States is better cared for than the dancer. The dancer very often tries to dance "through" an injury rather than taking the time to properly care for it. In the process of continuing to dance while injured the dancer favors the part, thereby placing increased stress,

Fig. 1-1. Few activities compare with dance in terms of the demands placed on the body.

tension, and strain on other parts of the body. This is followed in many cases by injury to those areas. All professionals who are associated with dance (dancers, teachers, and choreographers) should realize that every effort must be put forth to prevent and properly care for injuries.

Human beings have been concerned about traumatic injuries and disease since long before recorded time. The primitive tribesman would perish if an incapaciting injury or disease made him unable to forage for food or defend himself against hostile enemies. Out of a basic need for survival emerged the healing modalities of heat, massage, and therapeutic exercise. The soothing relief of hot springs or the warm sun rays became a common source of therapy for early man. Throughout the ages primitive and more sophisticated cultures alike found that rubbing of the body in a certain manner would bring about healing responses and that certain types of active movement could sometimes help an injured or diseased person return more quickly to normalcy. Soon specialists in healing methods became important officials of early cultures. These medicine men, or shamans, had as their primary duty the preventing of illness through rituals and the treating of the ill and incapacitated by the use of selected therapeutic techniques. Usually associated with injury and disease were fear and superstition. The shamans soon realized that faith was just as much a part of healing as application of therapeutic techniques. A comparison of past and current practices shows that not much has changed in healing approaches; the only real change has come about in the degree of sophistication and complication in care for injuries.

Current approaches in the care of traumatic injuries are primarily designed to assist nature in its normal healing process. These approaches can be listed as preventive conditioning, immediate care, follow-up care, and supportive techniques.

Preventive conditioning

In the last few years, preventive conditioning has become increasingly important to the sports world. Instead of being most concerned after an injury has occurred, organized sports has emphasized prevention of injuries "before the fact." Athletics has found that injuries can be decreased by the employment of proper conditioning methods. Preventive conditioning is concerned with obtaining a balance between strength, flexibility, and endurance. To prevent injury there must be a general high level of strength throughout the body, with more strength available than is required to minimally execute a given skill. However, overspecialization of strength development must be avoided. In other words, strength should not be developed just for a particular skill but should be acquired so that prime movers and assisters are equally balanced in strength with opposing muscles. The old saying "a person is only as strong as his weakest link" can certainly be applied to muscular strength. Flexibility is also a major factor in the prevention of injury, but it should never be developed at the expense of good muscle tone. Dancers often attempt to exceed anatomical limitations in their desire to become more flexible, and in doing so they often neglect strength in a specific area, which eventually may lead to joint disease. When considering preventive conditioning, endurance cannot be underestimated. "Staying power" of the dancer means the ability to withstand fatigue and engage in arduous activity over a long period of time. It is of the utmost importance to the dancer engaged in a performance that demands a high level of precision and energy output to remain as fresh at the end of the performance as at the beginning.

The concept of preventive conditioning is as important for the time a dancer is actually performing as it is for rehearsing or studying. Those involved in athletics are becoming more cognizant of the fact that the physical training that prepares an athlete for a particular sport is not enough to sustain the athlete throughout the season, since the sport itself does not normally maintain the level of conditioning required for optimum performance throughout a complete season. Consequently, there is a need for specialized conditioning two or three times a week to maintain the level of conditioning that the athlete brought to the beginning of the sport season. This concept applies to dancers as well as athletes. A dancer should engage in a daily technique class when performing. This technique class should be particularly concerned with a balance of strength in all the major muscles of the body as well as flexibility and endurance activities.

Immediate care

Often it is asked how a person got back into physical activity so fast following a serious sprain or strain. The answer to this question is many faceted. A highly conditioned body heals more quickly than a poorly conditioned one. Also the individual who is seriously involved in a physical endeavor is highly motivated to get well and thus responds well to physical therapy and medical treatment. Besides these two factors, the most important factor in the response of healing is the immediacy of proper care. For example, the application of cold, pressure, and elevation immediately following the injury may mean the difference between one and several weeks of recovery time.

Follow-up care

Effective follow-up care of an injury involves knowing when to apply various superficial and deep physical therapy modalities and when to employ exercise, both generally for the entire body and specifically with therapeutic exercise. Each injury has certain individual characteristics and must be treated according to its own peculiarities; however, general concepts can be applied. For example, it is desirable that an injured dancer engage in general physical activity without aggravating the injured part. The continuance of an exercise program encourages injury healing and decreases the possibility of severe scarring. However, this does not mean that a dancer should use the injured part before it is ready. A unique therapeutic strategy can be applied for each person and each injury type.

Supportive techniques

In the last 10 years the use of supportive techniques in athletics has greatly increased. Strapping, special wraps, and padding can assist tremendously in the protection and healing process of many injuries if they are applied properly and at the appropriate time. Many strapping techniques protect a part against additional injury and allow the dancer to engage more freely in general physical activity. Properly applied pads often can provide dancers with relief from pain and allow them to return to dancing faster than they could otherwise.

part two

The causes
of dance injury

Part 2 concerns the primary reasons why dancers become injured. Discussed in detail are body composition and how dancers use their bodies in ways that increase their susceptibility to trauma and other serious problems.

chapter two

Body structure
and composition

The active person sustains traumatic injuries by overstretching or abnormally compressing the body's tissues. These forces can result in injuries such as muscle strains, joint sprains, or even the more serious conditions of dislocations or fractures. Those qualities that allow the dancer's body to move freely and gracefully can also produce susceptibility to a variety of injuries. Although the body has a great deal of structural strength, it also possesses many structural weaknesses that, when subjected to abnormal stress, can lead to injury.

Joints

Whether the movable joints of the body are strong or weak depends on the strength of their skeletal, ligamentous, and muscular organization (Figs. 2-1 and 2-2). Although most are not, a joint ideally should be strong in all three anatomical aspects. The ankle is one such joint. The fibula and tibia form a cuplike mortise over the talus, and little movement is allowed in the ankle other than flexion and extension. The ligaments that help to bind the ankle joint provide strong support on its medial (inner) aspect but much less support on its

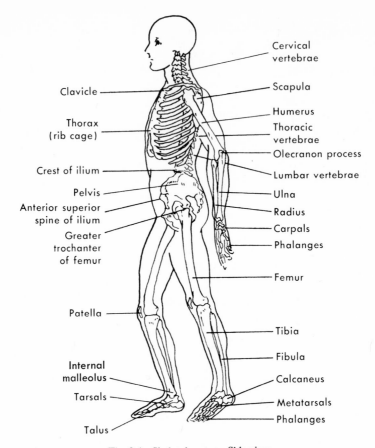

Clavicle

Thorax
(rib cage)

Crest of ilium

Pelvis

Anterior superior
spine of ilium

Greater
trochanter
of femur

Patella

Internal
malleolus

Tarsals

Talus

Cervical
vertebrae

Scapula

Humerus

Thoracic
vertebrae

Olecranon process

Lumbar vertebrae

Ulna

Radius

Carpals

Phalanges

Femur

Tibia

Fibula

Calcaneus

Metatarsals

Phalanges

Fig. 2-1. Skeletal system. Side view.

lateral (outer) aspect. In general the weakest factor in the ankle joint is its musculature because, with the exception of the calf muscle tendon or heel cord, the long tendons that cross all sides of the joint provide little strength. This anatomical weakness is the reason why ankle sprains are slow to rehabilitate and why, once disruption of supportive tissue has occurred, stability must be provided by outside elements such as special wraps or strappings.

The knee is designed to produce a hinge action. However, its skeletal makeup, in contrast to that of the ankle, is very weak; only a shallow recess is provided for each femoral condyle (articulating surface of the thigh bone) to rest on. Nature has assisted knee stability by providing two cartilaginous oval pieces that, like the discs between the vertebrae, assist in shock absorption and that also provide a slightly deeper socket for the femoral condyles. The knee, like the

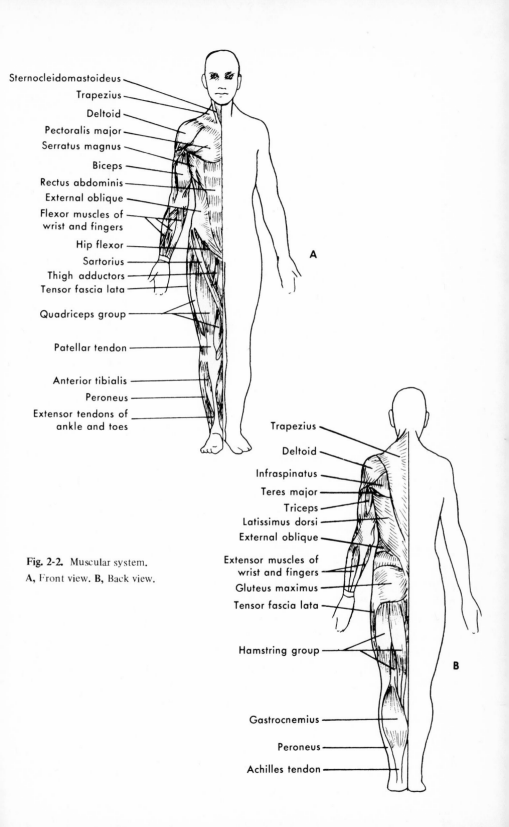

Sternocleidomastoideus
Trapezius
Deltoid
Pectoralis major
Serratus magnus
Biceps
Rectus abdominis
External oblique
Flexor muscles of
wrist and fingers
Hip flexor
Sartorius
Thigh adductors
Tensor fascia lata

Quadriceps group

Patellar tendon

Anterior tibialis
Peroneus
Extensor tendons of
ankle and toes

A

Trapezius
Deltoid
Infraspinatus
Teres major
Triceps
Latissimus dorsi
External oblique
Extensor muscles of
wrist and fingers
Gluteus maximus
Tensor fascia lata

Hamstring group

B

Gastrocnemius
Peroneus
Achilles tendon

Fig. 2-2. Muscular system.
A, Front view. B, Back view.

ankle, has its greatest ligamentous strength on its inner aspect (provided by the medial collateral ligaments), with a lighter and less dense ligamentous arrangement on the outer aspect. The knee is provided anterior-posterior (front-to-back) stabilization by the cruciate ligaments. However, by far the greatest strength of the knee joint comes from its musculature. Muscles such as the quadriceps group, which extends the knee; the hamstring group, which flexes the knee; and the gastrocnemius muscles, which primarily point the toes and assist in bending the leg, all provide the knee joint with great stability if conditioned properly.

The hip joint is extremely important to the dancer. Anatomically it is the strongest joint in the body. A deep socket for the head of the femur provides a strong skeletal organization together with a heavy network of ligamentous and fibrous tissue that completely surrounds the hip joint. The support provided by this arrangement is increased by many strong intrinsic and extrinsic muscles. Basically the hip is extremely strong in all its anatomical features and is able to withstand a great many of the stresses placed on it by dance. However, it should be noted that the hip is particularly vulnerable to injury in the flexed position. In flexion the hip joint loses stability and the articular capsule becomes lax, increasing its susceptibility to injury when placed in a stretch position, as in going from passé to extension.

The vertebral spine consists of many bones that, when combined, allow the trunk to move in many different directions. The areas of the spine most vulnerable to dance injury are the lumbosacral junction at the base of the vertebral column and the lumbar vertebrae located below the rib cage. When discussing the lumbosacral junction, we must consider the fact that at this point the movable spine makes contact with the very immovable pelvis. In general the lumbar spine can be weak or strong, depending on the balance of musculature in the lower abdomen and low back. The five lumbar vertebrae represent a strong skeletal and ligamentous structure but, like the lumbosacral, they are vulnerable to injury when weakness of the abdominal muscles is combined with tightness in the low back region. Body mechanics plays an extremely important role in the prevention of low back injuries and in determining whether or not the vertebral column and the pelvis are in good alignment.

The cervical region, or neck, does not have a very high incidence of injury in dance; however, occasionally a sudden twist or thrust will produce a muscle spasm or strain in this area. The cervical vertebrae are designed for full mobility. Consequently, they are not supported by a heavy bony design or ligamentous network. The greatest strength of the neck comes from its musculature. Therefore, if the muscles of the neck are not conditioned properly, they are prone to strain. Because the head, which sometimes weighs as much as 15 pounds, may be moved suddenly and with great force in any direction, the neck musculature can be easily overstretched.

Like the neck region, the shoulder girdle (which encompasses the articulations of the clavicle, the scapula, and the head of the humerus, or shoulder joint) is designed for full mobility and not support. The shoulder girdle gains its greatest strength from its musculature. Dance injuries of the shoulder girdle are primarily in the nature of sudden unrestrained muscle contractions.

Joints of the elbow, wrist, and hand do not have the same incidence of dance injury as other joints. However, they may hurt by a fall on the outstretched arm. The elbow is a strong joint in every aspect with the exception of the radial joint, which allows movement of the forearm. The wrist derives its greatest strength from ligaments and muscle tendons.

The propelling force of the human body comes from its motor system, which includes the nerves and muscles. To be effective, muscles under conscious control of the brain must contract and extend in synchrony, working reciprocally with their opposing muscles. Opposing muscles that do not relax effectively produce stress and tension in opposite muscles, thereby eventually resulting in pathologic conditions. Poorly trained or fatigued muscles have a tendency not to work reciprocally. Under these conditions, muscles strain easily. Muscles also pad the body with their bulk, providing to the underlying structures protection against contusions or blows from sources external to the body.

The human body is mechanically designed for sustained and accurate movement. The upright posture of the human being provides the opportunity for the arms to work freely, since they are not necessary for support of the upper body as in the four-legged animal. The human body cannot be said to be designed for great feats of strength, but for precision in fine and sensitive types of movement. Therefore one must set forth the premise that when the dancer does not use the body according to its major design, injury is imminent.

Postural implications

Good body mechanics is essential for efficient movement and defense against injury (Fig. 2-3). Body mechanics is defined as "the functional relationship between the various body parts." For effective movement, each segment of the body must be in proper relationship to adjacent segments. With good posture, the body functions with the least amount of stress that is possible for each movement and for each body type. Good body mechanics is relative to the type of activity being engaged in, such as sitting, standing, walking, and dancing, as well as to the type of body build with which the individual is endowed. Consequently, there is no normal posture that fits every individual. To maintain

Fig. 2-3. A, Good body mechanics is essential for efficient movement and defense against injury. **B,** Faulty body mechanics results in inefficient movement and a susceptibility to injury.

proper alignment the human body must continually combat the force of gravity as it is being pulled toward the center of the earth. Body segments that are misaligned react to gravity more adversely than segments that are in good alignment. In essence, proper body mechanics reflects good balance and a small amount of strain on the supporting and moving structures.

The center of gravity of the human body is also an essential factor in good postural alignment. This center is usually found at a point in the middle of the pelvis, approximately dividing the individual in half. Men normally have longer legs and a higher center of gravity, while women normally have shorter lower

B

Fig. 2-3, cont'd. For legend see opposite page.

limbs and a lower center of gravity. Standing upright on the two feet provides a very small base of support; consequently, the body is relatively unstable in its normal standing position. Either standing in one position or moving, the body is always striving to offset the pull of gravity. It is obvious, therefore, that the most stable position of the body is when it is aligned over its own base of support. The closer the body's center of gravity is to the center of its base of support, the better the equilibrium. Body movement is often the purposeful gaining and losing of the base of support. As indicated by Doris Humphrey, "In the human animal, the walk is the key pattern of fall and recovery, my theory of motion—that is, the giving in to and rebound from gravity. This is the very core of all movement, in my opinion. All life fluctuates between the resistance to and the yielding to gravity."*

Besides the reciprocal relationship of ligaments and muscles, there are many other factors within the human organism that are designed to maintain postural alignment. For example, postural positioning in dynamic movement is controlled by visual cues in terms of the body's position in space. The semicircular canals in the inner ear provide information on the dancer's body position to the brain. There are also receptors in the tendons, joints, and muscles that provide continual information to the brain and proprioceptors as to the body's relative position in space. Any malfunction of these organs individually or in relationship to one another can result in temporary problems or eventually cause serious postural malalignments and loss of movement efficiency, followed by an increased susceptibility to injury and eventual chronic orthopedic problems in later life. To the dancer, good postural alignment is essential for career longevity and freedom from acute and chronic handicapping injuries.

Good standing posture

As described, good posture in an efficient body and motor system allows for the maximum functioning of the body with expenditure of the least energy. Although the body is seldom in a static position, posture is often discussed in this way to provide examples of good alignment (Fig. 2-4). In the standing position the body weight is equally spread over the feet, with equal pressure placed on the various parts of the foot such as the heel and the ball of the foot. The five toes provide some assistance in the equalization of pressure. Balanced equally over the feet are the lower legs, which sit comfortably on top of the axis of each ankle, called the talus. Although the legs are straight, the knees are not maintained in a stiff or locked position. On top of the legs is the pelvis, balanced in such a manner that the muscles of the abdomen, lower back, and thighs are in equal contraction. The pelvis in coordination with the lumbar spine allows for a normal amount of anterior-posterior curvature. The upper back, supported primarily by the thoracic vertebrae, also has the proper amount of anterior-posterior curvature to be balanced with the lower lumbar spine. Resting comfortably on the thorax is the shoulder girdle, with the arm hanging in a straight line down the sides of the trunk. Sitting on top of the cervical spine, the head is positioned in such a manner that its weight is distributed equally in front and in back. In such a balanced position the jaw is at right angles to the floor.

---

*From Humphrey, D.: The art of making dances, New York, 1959, Rinehart & Co., Inc.

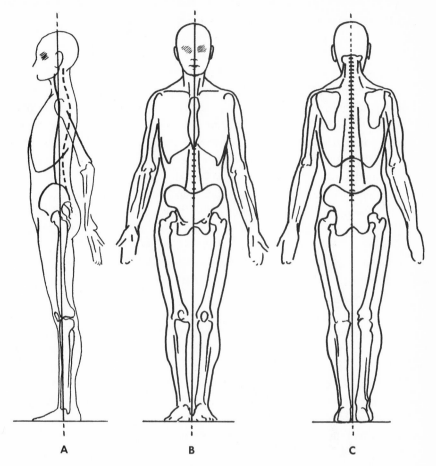

Fig. 2-4. Normal postural alignment. **A,** Side view. **B,** Front view. **C,** Back view.

The best method to determine standing posture is by employing the plumb line test, with a weighted string extending the full length of the body.

Ideally, when viewed from the lateral (side) position, a person who has good posture alignment would have the following postural features. With the plumb line hanging the full length of the body, the line would cross from just behind the ear, through the center of the shoulder, through the middle of the pelvis, through the center of the hip, just in back of the kneecap, and just in front of the ankle bone. One must also scrutinize the arm hang. The arm should hang loosely from the shoulder, with the hand resting comfortably at the center of the hip.

Good posture from the front view can be determined by a horizontal-vertical reference point. Vertically the plumb line should cross evenly through the entire length of the body, starting in the center of the head, passing down the middle of the nose, mouth, chest, abdomen (or linea alba), and umbilicus, and extending between the two legs. Horizontally the shoulder tips should line up with one another; the nipple line should be even; the top of the hips, or the ilium, should be in line; and the kneecaps should be aligned. One can also look at the arm hang in the front position to determine whether the arms are equal in length. It is also important to determine leg alignment from the front view. To do so the plumb line is dropped from the anterior-superior spine of the ilium, crossing the middle of the kneecap and striking the apex of the instep.

From the rear view one also must look at vertical and horizontal lines to determine normal postural alignment. Vertically a plumb line is taken from the center of the head. The line should then cross the center of the spine, falling between the buttocks and striking the floor so that the feet are of equal distance from the plumb line. The back view can also indicate to the observer whether the shoulders are level and if the scapulae are in horizontal alignment.

Of extreme importance to the entire body is the proper alignment of the foot, ankle, and leg (Figs. 2-5 and 2-6). Like the other segmental relationships of the body, the foot and ankle must be properly aligned if the complicated system of tendons and muscles is to work efficiently. Because the foot is the base of support for the entire body, faulty alignment here can cause postural deviations in the other mechanical systems of the body. An ideal relationship of the bony segments of the foot and leg produces the maximum efficiency during standing and locomotion. In the standing posture the lower third of the leg rests on the talus, which in turn rests directly on the heel bone, or calcaneus. The talus and the calcaneus represent the hindfoot, or tarsus. The midfoot, or lesser tarsus, consists of the navicular, cuboid, and three cuneiform bones; the five metatarsals and the five phalanges constitute the forefoot. In movement in the upright position, weight is transferred forward on the foot to the three cuneiform bones and the cuboid and then to the metatarsals and phalanges. In the normal standing position the body weight is carried on the heel and the forefoot, with weight being distributed equally throughout the heads of the five metatarsal bones. The toes also assist in balancing the body by having their bottom surfaces fully in contact with the floor.

The foot also has several arches that provide for normal functioning and protection. Longitudinal arches are found on the medial and lateral aspects of the foot. The inside or medial longitudinal arch extends from the anterior aspect of the heel to the distal heads of the metatarsal bones, while the normally smaller lateral longitudinal arch extends from the heel to the distal head of the

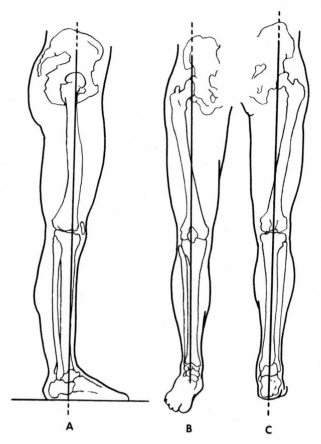

Fig. 2-5. Normal leg and foot alignment. **A,** Side view. **B,** Front view. **C,** Back view.

fifth metatarsal. An extremely important arch in the forepart of the foot is the metatarsal arch, which is dome shaped and formed by the front heads of the metatarsal bones. In general a healthy foot is one that is well articulated and flexible and has strong ligaments and good muscle tone. For the dancer the normally aligned foot is one of the most important physical assets.

Common postural problems

From birth to death the human organism is resisting the force of gravity. The newborn baby lying in the crib is almost completely overcome by the pressure of gravity and unable to do anything but lie in a recumbent position. As the musculature and skeletal system mature, the infant is eventually able to overcome gravity and assume an upright posture. Gravity is continually forcing

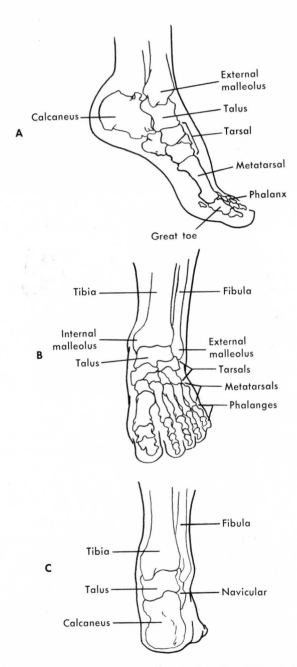

Fig. 2-6. Proper bony relationships of the foot. **A,** Side view. **B,** Front view. **C,** Back view.

the individual toward the center of the earth. The ultimate upright posture demands specific strength of major antigravity muscles such as the erector muscles of the spine (erector spinae), the quadriceps group, and the gastrocnemius. Ideally the mature person resists gravity through symmetrical and synchronous muscular development. When improper use of the body is undertaken before there is physiological readiness to withstand the rigors of a particular stressful activity (which sometimes happens in ballet), the body will assume faulty habits.

Dance, like any strenuous, repetitious activity, can provide the performer with an outstanding opportunity to develop a well-conditioned body. On the other hand, if dance movements are engaged in improperly or movements are attempted that are beyond a dancer's ability level, the result may be a breakdown of supporting structures followed by serious postural deviations or injury.

Screening for postural deviations

All persons concerned with dance should have an understanding of basic screening methods in determining body alignment and misalignment. The most common techniques utilized for screening postural alignment are the grid, the plumb line, and various special devices to determine leg, ankle, and foot alignment.

The posture grid (Fig. 2-7) is composed of a network of 4-inch squares or 6-inch rectangles suspended on an angular frame 7½ feet long and 3 feet wide. Down the center of the grid, dividing it equally in half, is a line, usually of a different color or width. This center line is equivalent to a plumb line. The vertical and horizontal lines of the posture screen provide various reference points. In determining body segment alignment or misalignment, the inspector can observe the dancer either as a total entity or in segments.

In using the posture screen the inspector should have the dancer wear as little clothing as possible. The typical dance costume of leotards and tights is excellent for scanning the contours of the body, but when it comes to observing the back, shoulders, and legs, it is desirable to have the skin revealed. The dancer is screened from three views: the side, back, and front. For the observation the dancer takes a position approximately 12 inches behind the screen and stands so that the center line of the grid crosses the midline of the body. The dancer's feet are then positioned with the heels approximately 2 inches apart and the feet slightly abducted (turned out). In the side view the dancer stands so that the center line of the screen strikes just in front of the lateral malleolus (ankle bone). In the back view position the dancer stands with his back to the screen approximately 12 inches from the screen with his heels 2 inches apart and feet slightly turned out. The dancer is instructed to stand as naturally as possible while being viewed.

Postural deviations that are determined by reading the grid are normally indicated in terms of mild, modest, or severe or in degrees of deviation. When viewing the entire body as a whole, 1 degree is equivalent to 2 inches in

Fig. 2-7. Determining postural deviations through the use of a grid.

deviation. When observing segmental alignment, on the other hand, 1 degree represents 1 inch of deviation.

The inspector normally stands approximately 12 feet from the dancer, who is behind the screen. From this distance the entire body can be seen. While the dancer takes each of the three prescribed positions, the inspector first looks at the entire body for leaning and whole body distortion and then views the body segmentally, either from foot to head or vice versa. The relationships are of the head to the shoulder, the trunk to the pelvis, the pelvis to the thigh, and the thigh to the lower leg. It should be understood that the posture grid method for determining postural anomalies gives only an indication of gross or obvious inadequacies and should not be used as a definitive diagnostic tool. The static

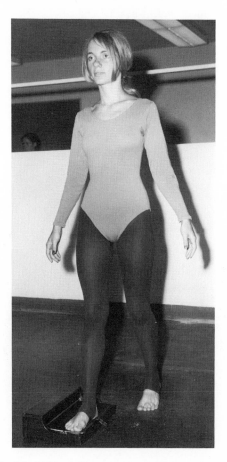

Fig. 2-8. Taking a foot impression on the pedograph.

standing position that is assumed behind the screen is not typical of a human attitude; therefore extreme caution should be taken by the observer when making definitive statements as to the seriousness of specific postural divergencies. The plumb line is an excellent tool in determining lateral deviations, front midline deviations, and back midline deviations. It is also valuable in determining vertical leg alignment.

The foot examination is more difficult than screening other segments of the body. However, there are two tests that can be utilized by the layman to determine proper alignment of the foot and ankle.* These tests, although not equivalent to examination by a physician, can indicate to the observer conditions that may need further examination. The first of the instruments used is the pedograph (Fig. 2-8). The pedograph print is similar to a fingerprint except that it is of the foot under weight-bearing conditions. The subject is instructed

---

*More detailed foot tests can be found in Arnheim, D. D., Auxter, D., and Crowe, W. C.: Principles and methods of adapted physical education, ed. 2, St. Louis, 1973, The C. V. Mosby Co.

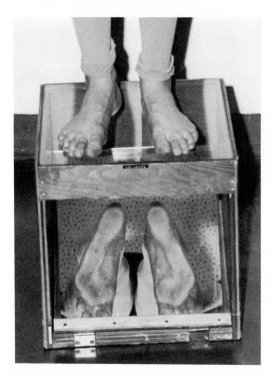

Fig. 2-9. Weight-bearing characteristics indicated by the pedoscope.

to walk up to the pedograph and step on it in a normal manner. The pedograph in turn makes an ink impression of the foot on a paper recording form. Although not a definitive screening device that would normally be used in medicine, this device does reveal weight-bearing characteristics and indicates the position of the toes, the relative height of the longitudinal arch, and the relative position of the metatarsal arch.

Another excellent tool is the pedoscope (Fig. 2-9). It is normally a boxlike device made of wood with a ½-inch glass top and a reflecting mirror inside. The subject stands on the glass top while pressure from the weight bearing is reflected in the mirror for observation by the examiner. Weight-bearing areas are reflected as pale white areas. Besides weight bearing, the examiner can also observe a number of other foot features, namely, the general position of the longitudinal and the metatarsal arches and the relationship of the Achilles tendon to the calcaneus. The observer also can readily see if there is abnormal callus formation on the foot.

Postural problems in dance

There are many postural deviations that are obvious from the side view. These deviations are more technically called anterior-posterior deviations. The first and probably most common is forward head. In this situation the ear appears in front of the plumb line rather than in good alignment. The individual who is constantly in this abnormal position develops weakness in the extensor cervical muscles that keep the head erect and develops a shortening of the flexor muscles in the front of the neck. Occasionally the forward head becomes incorrectly realigned by development of cervical lordosis, or accentuation of the normal curve of the neck (Fig. 2-10). In this situation the dancer would appear to have normal alignment except that the chin would jut upward instead of being parallel to the floor.

Fig. 2-10. Cervical lordosis.

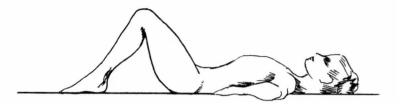

Fig. 2-11. Neck and back flattening exercise to correct forward head and cervical lordosis. Lying on the back with knees bent, the dancer first flattens the neck, then the shoulders, and then the lower back. Holding this flattened position, the dancer slowly tries to straighten the legs without reestablishing the spinal curves.

Fig. 2-12. Kyphosis of the thoracic spine.

Fig. 2-13. Side arm raise exercise to correct conditions of the upper trunk. Lying on a floor or bench facing downward, the dancer raises the arms to the side, attempting to touch the shoulder blades together.

Fig. 2-14. Lumbar lordosis.

In correcting forward head the dancer must strenghthen the extensor muscles of the neck, stretch the flexors, and learn to maintain the proper position. It is suggested that the dancer try to push the head upward as if a rod were holding the head on top of the shoulders. Correction of cervical lordosis can be attained by much the same procedure; however, the dancer must attempt to decrease the curve of the neck by going through various neck and back flattening exercises (Fig. 2-11).

Moving downward from the head and neck, the examiner next scans the thorax and shoulder complex. A common deviation in this area is forward shoulders, in which the shoulders are forward of the plumb line. In this situation there is muscular tightness in the chest region and a stretching and weakening of the muscles in the upper back region. Often associated with forward shoulders are winged scapulae, caused by the scapulae being pulled outward from the rib cage.

A more serious condition in the upper trunk region, often associated with forward shoulders, is an exaggerated spinal curve called kyphosis (Fig. 2-12). Kyphosis of the thoracic spine is an abnormal rounding of the upper back that produces much the same type of muscular imbalance seen in forward shoulders: tight musculature in the chest that overpowers the weaker muscles of the upper back, particularly the erector spinae muscles, which maintain the spine in an erect position. Overcoming these conditions of the upper trunk requires a stretching and lengthening of the musculature in the chest region and a strengthening of the erector spinae muscles and the posterior aspect of the shoulder girdle (Fig. 2-13).

Lumbar lordosis is a common postural deviation of the lumbar spine and pelvis in which the normal forward curve of the lumbar spine is accentuated (Fig. 2-14). This condition often results in a forward tilting of the pelvis, adding to the swaybacked appearance that is characteristic of many dancers. Because this area is very near the center of gravity, there are many muscles involved. Normally the pelvis is maintained in its balanced position by an even pull of the abdominal and lumbosacral muscles together with the muscles of the thigh and hip. However, in lumbar lordosis the abdominal muscles are weaker than the muscles of the lumbar spine, which are usually contracted and tight, and the hamstring muscles. Also, in lordosis the rectus femoris muscles of the quadriceps group are usually tight. This muscular imbalance results in the pulling down of the pelvis anteriorly, creating the typical swayback or forward pelvic tilt. Overcoming lordosis requires a great deal of hard work involving stretching the low back and hip flexors and strengthening the hamstring and abdominal muscles in

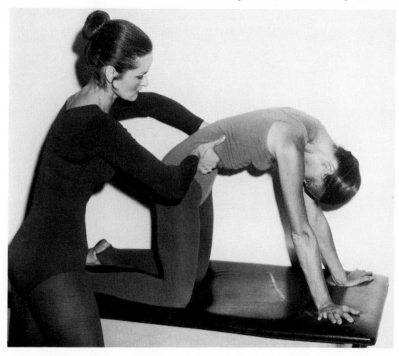

Fig. 2-15. Mad cat exercise for lumbar lordosis. Taking a four-point position, the dancer drops the head down, rounds the upper back, flattens the lower back by contracting the abdominal and buttock muscles, and then moves to a straight spine position.

a concerted effort to reestablish lumbar, pelvic, and leg alignment (Fig. 2-15).

Flat back is a condition opposite to lordosis in terms of specific muscle imbalances. It results in a flattening of the low back and a posterior (backward) tilt of the pelvis (Fig. 2-16). Correction of flat back involves strengthening of the low back and hip flexors and stretching the abdominal and hamstring muscles.

Closely associated with the relative position of the pelvis and vertebral column are the thigh and lower legs. As described earlier, a normal lateral alignment of the legs is when the plumb line falls from the center of the hip, crossing just behind the patella and just in front of the outer malleolus. A plumb line that falls in front of the patella may reveal a condition called back knees, or genu recurvatum (Fig. 2-17, *A*). This problem is very closely associated with lordosis and the forward tilt of the pelvis frequently found in ballet dancers. Back knee is produced by an imbalance in the strength of the quadriceps, hamstring, and gastrocnemius muscles. The gastrocnemius and quadriceps

Fig. 2-16. Flat back.

overpower the hamstrings, pulling the leg and thigh back into a hyperextended position. To overcome back knee a great deal of effort must be expended to realign the hip, thigh, and lower leg, with special attention given to strengthening the hamstrings.

On the other hand, if the plumb line falls well behind the patella, the knee is in a hyperflexed position, indicating tight and constricted hamstring muscles (Fig. 2-17, *B*). In contrast to treating back knee, the hamstrings of the hyperflexed knee should be stretched and lengthened to restore the proper alignment. The hyperflexed knee is most often characteristic of the individual with flat back.

The student of posture must be aware that a deviation in any one segment of

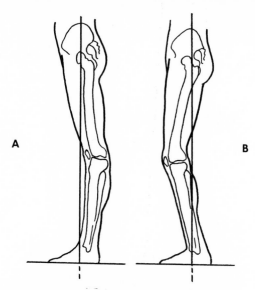

Fig. 2-17. Side view of leg malalignments. **A,** Back knees. **B,** Hyperflexed knees.

the body can produce additional deviations in many other parts of the body. For example, a dancer with chronic forward head could develop forward shoulders, kyphosis, lordosis, and hyperextended knees as the result of this one deviation.

In viewing the body from the front, the observer should study both the vertical and horizontal components. Scanning the body in its entirety should determine if there is a left or right tilt. Body tilting may be the result of faulty habits or of a shortened leg (Fig. 2-18).

Studying the segments of the body from head to foot, the observer may find many deviations common in dancers. In relationship to the shoulders the head may be tilted left or right or it may be twisted. Head tilt, as with whole body tilt, demands a reeducation of the proper sense of positioning. In the more severe cases, reeducation must be combined with a proper exercise program that includes stretching of the contracted side and strengthening of the elongated side of the neck. Viewing the body from the front can reveal many aberrations of the shoulders, shoulder girdle, and arms. For example, one shoulder can be higher than the other or both shoulders can be abnormally high because of contracted musculature on both sides of the upper shoulder region. Shoulders that are uneven or asymmetrical can result from a curvature in the spine or can occur because of some abnormality within the shoulder complex. If the origin of deviation is within the shoulder musculature, it is important that the contracted

Fig. 2-18. Forward body tilt.

side be stretched and the lower side be strengthened along with reeducation exercises. Specific distortions of the trunk can be discerned by such signs as an uneven nipple line or an off-center linea alba (center line created by the coming together of the abdominal muscles). An uneven hang of the arms may indicate to the observer an abnormal deviation of the thorax and vertebral column.

A lateral pelvic tilt, a condition in which the pelvis is low on one side and high on the other, can be detected from both the front and back views. This condition is usually associated with contracted muscles in the low back attributed to uneven leg length. Kneecaps that are not level often reveal a shortening of one leg. This type of asymmetry should be routinely referred to a physician for a more accurate assessment and remediation. Front view screening is best for determining leg alignment because key landmarks such as the anterior

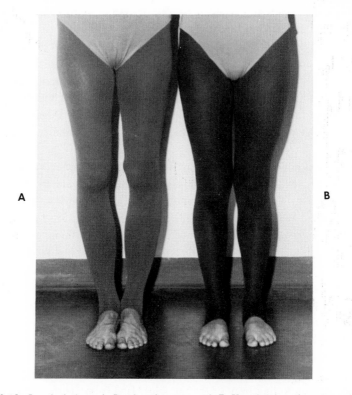

Fig. 2-19. Leg deviations. **A,** Bowlegs (genu varum). **B,** Knock-knees (genu valgum).

superior spine of the ilium, the kneecap, and the foot are more easily discerned from the front.

There are three leg deviations common to dancers. These are tibial torsion (a twisting of the lower leg bones), knock-knee, or genu valgum (Fig. 2-19, *A*), and bowlegs, or genu varum (Fig. 2-19, *B*). Tibial torsion is best determined by examining the position of the kneecap. In most cases the kneecap of the dancer with tibial torsion is rotated inward with the foot pointing straight ahead. Less often the foot is pointed straight ahead while the kneecap is rotated outward. Because this is a condition involving the entire leg, correction involves the ankle, knee, and hip. Commonly the outward rotators of the hip and thigh are weak in comparison to the inward rotators, which are tight and need to be stretched. Dancers with this problem should be identified early and referred to a specialist for shoe correction and remedial exercises. This condition can be caused by the young dancer performing pliés incorrectly with the knee turned inward and the foot outward.

Both knock-knees and bowlegs are determined in terms of how the legs are aligned. The knock-kneed dancer displays the ability to touch the medial femoral condyles (insides of the knees) but is unable to touch the insides of the ankle bones. In this situation the lower legs are abducted (turned out from the midline of the body). On the other hand, the dancer who has bowlegs is unable to touch the insides of the knees while touching together the insides of the ankles. This produces a bowed appearance in the legs. Where there is a separation either at the ankles or the inside of the knees, 1 degree represents each inch of separation.

Often associated with bowlegs are high longitudinal arches, supinated ankles with feet inverted, hyperextended knees, and an inward rotation of the thighs. Conversely, with knock-knees the longitudinal arches are low, the ankles are often pronated with the feet everted, and there is an outward rotation of the thighs. In both bowlegs and knock-knees, correction should include proper shoeing and must be conducted early in life if remediation is to occur. Dancers who abnormally stress their bodies very early in life often develop lower limb deviations. An astute teacher of dance will make sure that all students are physically mature enough to withstand the physical rigors placed on them by particular techniques. It is of the utmost importance that an attempted dance skill is not deleterious to a child's normal postural development.

The most obvious postural anomalies that can be discerned from the back are the winged scapula and scoliosis. The winged scapula is a deviation that displays an abduction or pulling away of the shoulder blade from the thorax, producing a wing effect. This problem is very common among very thin dancers with a generally weak shoulder girdle and is often naturally overcome when the individual begins to use the arms in hanging and support activities. The winged scapula is often associated with forward shoulders and can be remedied by exercises that lengthen the chest muscles and strengthen the muscles that pull the scapula towards the spinal column (the rhomboid major muscles).

Scoliosis is the most serious of all postural deviations. It is a lateral deviation of the spinal column that causes an asymmetry of the thorax, pelvis, and upper and lower limbs. Curvature of the spine can be detected from the back view and appears as a "C" or "S" curve (Fig. 2-20). As was indicated in the discussion of the front view deviations, asymmetry that is produced by a scoliotic curve is often reflected in the front view by an uneven nipple line, uneven arm hang, and a linea alba that deviates left or right from the center posture screen line. There may also appear to be a lateral hip tilt. A "C" curve is commonly called a simple curve and, as all curves are indicated as to direction, it is named for its convex side. A "C" curve that has attempted to compensate for the deviation is commonly

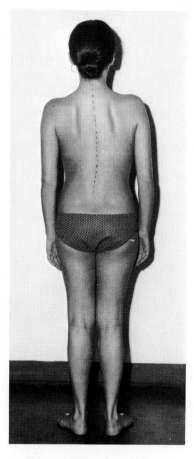

Fig. 2-20. "S"-curve scoliosis.

called an "S" curve. However, the "S" compensation is usually incomplete, leaving the dancer with a great deal of asymmetry throughout the body. Because the causes of the lateral spinal deviation are numerous, varied, and often unknown, it is usually not detected until the individual is in late childhood or early adolescence, often too late to make permanent corrections. In many cases the dance teacher will be the one to detect this type of problem and should immediately refer the student to a physician. In the early stages of scoliosis the primary problem is functional, involving only soft tissue, and can often be corrected by proper treatment. As the condition progresses, the problem becomes a combination of soft tissue and permanent skeletal and ligamentous changes that are difficult if not impossible to completely correct. Dance can be an outstanding means of ameliorating scoliosis because it demands an ability for symmetry of movement. Unilateral activities, particularly those that exert a strong pull on the side of the curve, should be avoided at all costs.

Several tests can be initiated by the screener to determine whether scoliosis is present. The first is to very carefully palpate and mark with a grease pencil each spinous process of the dancer. Observation of this line may reveal the presence of a curvature. If so, the dancer should bend forward from the waist, allowing the arms to hang down. Two factors are observed while the dancer is in this position: (1) whether the spine straightens out in this position and (2) whether the thorax appears to be elevated more on one side than the other. If the spine straightens out while the dancer is bent over, it may indicate that the problem is functional, or involving primarily soft muscle tissue. If the curve only partly straightens out, then the condition may be considered transitional, or consisting

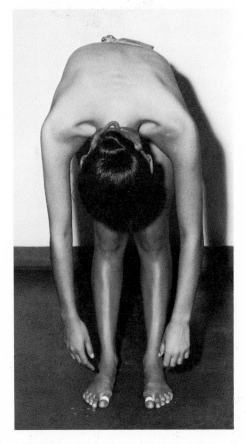

Fig. 2-21. Elevated right thorax in a dancer with scoliosis.

of a combination of pliable soft tissue and permanently curved bone structures. If there is no straightening, the problem may be completely fixated in deformed bone. If the rib cage is higher on one side, it may indicate a twisting of the thorax as a result of the lateral deviation of the spine (Fig. 2-21).

It is advisable to check the dancer's leg length when scoliosis is suspected or has been determined by the preceding examination. Uneven length of the long bones of the legs is a major indicator of scoliosis in late childhood and early adolescence. Although definitive determination of uneven leg length must come from a physician, the dance instructor can make a subjective observation of the problem and subsequently refer the dancer to the proper professional source. The test is given with the dancer lying in a supine position with legs together and arms at the sides. The examiner stands at the dancer's feet and grasps the dancer's ankles with palms resting just under the medial malleolus of each ankle. After pulling gently to completely lengthen the legs, the examiner determines whether the medial ankle bones are lined up. While both legs are being observed, the examiner also makes a determination of whether the patella and the anterior spine of the illium of each leg appear to be even.

Persons usually develop some asymmetry in their bodies because of hand dominance and the use of one side of the body in preference to the other. Therefore the majority of persons might be said to have some minor postural deviations contributing to scoliosis. However, to the dancer even the most minute asymmetry may eventually result in a serious acute injury or perhaps permanent chronic physical limitations and eventual elimination from the dance profession.

Foot malalignment and structural problems

It must be said that the feet and legs are the primary tools of dance and must function at their optimum level in order for them to be highly responsive to the will of the dancer. The feet are mentioned last in this chapter but are not considered least in importance because foot problems can be a detriment to the efficient functioning of the entire body. Painful feet can be devastating to the dancer's career. Consequently, it is necessary that problems of the feet, particularly mechanical defects, be overcome as soon as possible before permanent impairment occurs. Such factors as good hygiene, maintaining muscles in proper condition, and properly fitting shoes and socks are of the utmost importance to the person who desires to maintain his feet in top health.

Because of the great stress the dancer places on the feet, many common problems can arise. The first can be categorized as arch deviations. In general the arches of the foot provide proper positioning of various foot bones with important segments properly aligned to prevent overstretching of ligaments and ensure the normal functioning of muscles. The primary foot segments that should be kept in good position are the seven irregularly shaped tarsal bones, the five metatarsal bones, and the fourteen phalanx bones that make up the toes. These bones, the tibia and fibula (lower leg bones), and the talus bone of the ankle must be properly aligned in the static standing posture as well as in the dynamic locomotor postures. Arches provide a shock-absorbing protection to the rest of the body and also provide a space for tendons and other structures without being overly impinged on as the result of weight bearing. Ideally the dancer is seeking an extremely strong and flexible foot, which implies that bones are properly placed, ligaments are not abnormally stretched, and intrinsic and extrinsic muscles are in good tone. Contrary to what has been thought in the past, arches that have begun to fall cannot be restored to proper height with exercise. Therefore early signs of foot problems must be acted on before permanent structural deviations have taken place. Concern for the maintenance of arch integrity must be given when pain first arises.

Pes planus (flatfoot) refers to the lowering of the border of the medial longitudinal arch (Fig. 2-22). It occurs when, because of improper foot attire, excess weight, or improper use of the foot, the structures that had once provided stabilization allow the medial longitudinal arch to fall. This problem is very often associated with the pronated foot, knock-knees, and tibial torsion. Persons having this problem may toe-out in walking. Amelioration of pes planus involves elimination of its cause and strengthening of weakened muscles. Exercise that encourages a curling downward action of toes may help to prevent further dropping of the arch. With the falling of the longitudinal arch and the tendency of the foot to pronate, muscles on the lateral aspect of the foot, the peroneal group, tend to shorten along with the gastrocnemius and soleus muscles, which help to point the foot. The dancer with longitudinal arch problems should be discouraged from dancing on hard, rigid surfaces for long periods of time and encouraged to do activities on soft, resilient kinds of material such as grass or sand.

The opposite of pes planus is the problem of pes cavus (Fig. 2-23), or very high longitudinal arch. In this condition, abnormal stress is placed on the instep, ball of the foot, and the heel. Pes cavus is usually associated with heavy callus formation on the plantar aspect of the heel and the ball of the foot as a result of the increased stresses in these areas. If pain is associated with this problem, referral should be made to a foot specialist.

The pronated foot is often associated with ankle deviation; however, it is primarily within the forefoot and is a dual problem of foot abduction and

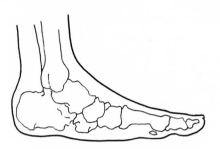

Fig. 2-22. Pes planus (flatfoot).

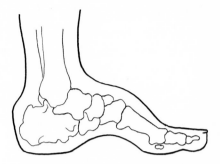

Fig. 2-23. Pes cavus (high arch).

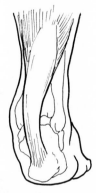

Fig. 2-24. Pronated foot with Helbing's sign.

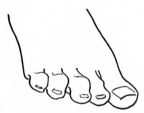

Fig. 2-25. Hammer toes.

eversion. In this problem there is a strain on the medial border of the longitudinal arch. This deviation also results in a faulty relationship of the talus, calcaneus and tarsal, and phalangeal articulations. Inspection from the rear of the pronated ankle often reveals a bowing medialward of the Achilles tendon. This condition is called Helbing's sign (Fig. 2-24). Prolonged pronation of the foot frequently produces other deviations such as knock-knees and deviations in the hip region. The opposite of the pronated foot is the supinated foot, which is often associated with bowlegs and pes cavus.

Other problems common to the foot are painful conditions that center about the metatarsal arch and the toes. For example, Morton's toe is a condition called true metatarsalgia in which there is a breakdown of the metatarsal arch, causing abnormal pressure on nerves at the ball of the foot. This pain also occurs often at the head of the fourth metatarsal as the result of being depressed and partially

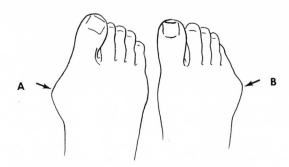

Fig. 2-26. Bunions. **A,** Hallux valgus. **B,** Tailor's bunion.

dislocated. Pressure on the plantar nerve produces a very painful neuritis along with disability. To alleviate the problem a special foot pad must be prepared and strategically placed to alleviate the painful pressure and reestablish the proper alignment of the metatarsal arch.

Hammer toes (Fig. 2-25) and crooked toes frequently occur as a result of shoes that are too narrow or too short. For maximum functioning, toes should be maintained in a straight position to efficiently propel the body by pressing or pushing against the supporting base. If the hammer toe or the crooked toe becomes painful, the only alternatives are specialized footwear or surgery to alleviate the disability.

Finally, but not least of the toe problems commonly found among dancers are hallux valgus and the tailor's bunion (Fig. 2-26). These problems are the result of shoes or socks that are too short or too narrow, producing abnormal pressure at the metatarsophalangeal joint of the great toe or the little toe. In dancers the cause may be dancing on pointe before there is adequate strength and joint maturation. In these cases an irritation results and an extra mineral accumulation occurs in the joint along with toe distortion, which in the great toe is away from and in the little toe is toward the midline of the body. Early detection of these problems is necessary, combined with proper precautions to prevent further irritation and deformity.

Good posture is essential to the dancer in preventing injuries. Good postural alignment reflects muscles that are in balance and functioning efficiently. Constant malalignment and faulty body positioning produce unbalances in opposing musculature. If this occurs over a long period of time, the supporting and moving structures become chronically imbalanced. In such situations the tissues in and about the area of imbalance are often not able to withstand the rigors of physical stress.

Morphologic variations in female and male dancers

It is obvious that there are great variances and dissimilarities in body morphology between male and female. The most common description of body morphology is the somatotype of *endomorph, mesomorph,* and *ectomorph.* The endomorph characteristically is obese, usually having little muscle tone with small bones, large head, long trunk, short neck, and short arms and legs with tapering digits. The endomorph also has sparse, fine hair as well as soft, smooth skin. The mesomorph has a well-defined skeletal structure with strong and highly toned muscles, a broad, sloping shoulder line and a slender waist, wide hips, and long arms and legs. The ectomorph, in contrast, has a very thin and narrow build with little muscle tone and long, underdeveloped arms and legs, usually with oversized hands and feet.

Most individuals, are mixtures of the three types of body build. The female build is less apt to fit one of these than is the male. The female body form is more mixed or dysplastic than the male; however, any body can be altered or modified to some extent through physical training from one body build type to another. Obviously there are movement performance advantages and disadvantages in having a certain somatotype. The most physically versatile somatotype is the mesomorph because of the ability to engage successfully in a great variety of physical activities. Least of these three types in terms of performance expectation is the endomorph. The problem of overweight combined with little muscle tone and strength makes the variety of movements demanded in dance more difficult.

Logically, performance expectations differ for men and women. The male is characteristically stronger than the female but has less balance. Greater strength in the male is due to the greater amount of the hormone testosterone that is secreted into the bloodstream. The female is generally weaker than the male and has a broader and shallower pelvis and a greater angle of the elbow. In the female pelvis there is a more acute hip angle, which produces less mechanical strength advantage in executing running and jumping activities. In activities that involve the arms, such as throwing or supporting the body, the female is usually at a disadvantage because her shoulders are narrower than those of the typical male and because she has a greater angle of the arm at the elbow, which provides less mechanical advantage. On the other hand, the mature female normally has a lower center of gravity than the male; therefore she has a greater potential for balance and stability.

Research points out that the male and female can work equally hard in physical activities without adverse effects. Contrary to past thinking, exercise is as beneficial to the girl or woman as to the boy or man. A girl should not fear the problem of developing unsightly bulging muscles from vigorous exercise programs. Bulging muscles are usually the result of abnormal and extensive overuse of a specific muscle group. With proper stretching and the equal exercise of antagonist muscles, this type of overdevelopment can be avoided. It is suggested that after performance of a movement pattern that contracts one set of muscles a pattern should be executed that uses the opposite set of muscles.

An additional factor that must be considered in the female dancer is her menstrual period. Although it was thought in the past that exercise should be avoided during the menstrual period, research now points out that vigorous activity usually causes no ill effects. Medical authorities suggest that when the womb is heavily engorged with blood during the first days of the menstrual period it is advisable to avoid jarring or sudden torque (twisting) movements.

chapter three

The dancer's body
correct use and misuse

Dancers often injure themselves as a result of taking improper or unnatural postures. They often attempt movements that are either beyond their particular capabilities or are inappropriate to their particular body build. Because dance is the epitome of motor control and physical endurance, inability to effectively extend oneself over a long period of time with good body mechanics eventually leads the dancer to sustain an acute or chronic injury.

Young dancers can become injured when attempting movements that are beyond their individual maturity levels. The dance teacher must deal with children at the level of their maturity. It must be realized, for example, that young children have muscles that are stronger than their bony attachments. Children, therefore, should only engage in those dance activities that are suited to their physical age and abilities.

As in sports, there are inherent dangers in dance that could lead to an injury for even the most cautious person. Poor timing, a faulty lift, and a poorly designed stage set are common factors contributing to dance injuries. The well-trained dancer moves on and off the stage with grace and poise that shows

45

Fig. 3-1. Plié in second position. **A,** Incorrect positioning. Abnormal stress is placed on the inside of the feet, ankles, knees, and hips. The shoulders and lower back do not form a straight line over the legs. **B,** Correct positioning. Each body segment is well balanced over the part below. Knees are over feet. Weight is distributed evenly over entire foot.

Fig. 3-2. Lifting a partner overhead. **A,** Incorrect positioning. The male dancer is leaning back too far, failing to properly distribute the weight of the female along his posture line. Abnormal stress is produced in the male dancer's neck and low back. **B,** Correct positioning. This lift is executed with the smallest amount of strain possible. The female dancer's center of gravity and body weight fall in a straight line along the balanced posture of the male dancer.

efficient positioning of all the segments of the body. Every form of dance requires good form and technique. Faulty technique and body placement eventually result in muscle strain, a tendency toward joint sprain, and an inability to effectively withstand chronic stresses applied to the body. Figs. 3-1 to 3-6 show correct use and misuse of the body in common dance positions.

There is no endeavor in life that can place the demands on the human organism that are placed on it by dance. Dance in itself develops positive mental and physical attributes; however, the rigors of dance can countermand these

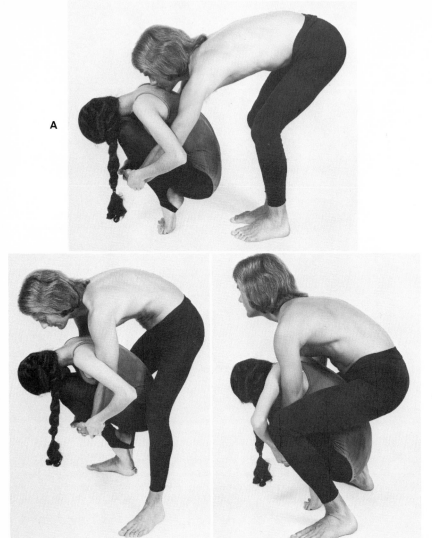

Fig. 3-3. Lifting a partner from the floor. **A,** Incorrect positioning. The female dancer is positioned too far out from her partner's center of gravity, placing unnecessary stress on the male dancer's low back. **B,** Incorrect positioning. The position of the male is better here than in **A.** However, it is still injury producing because his back is rounded, his knees are too straight, and the weight of the partner is in front of his center of gravity. **C,** Correct positioning. The position in **C** is less injury producing than either **A** or **B** because the head of the male dancer is raised, the back is straighter, the knees are bent, and the major weight of the female dancer is more directly under the hips of her partner. In this initial position the lift is mainly executed by the strength of the thighs, placing little stress on the back and shoulders.

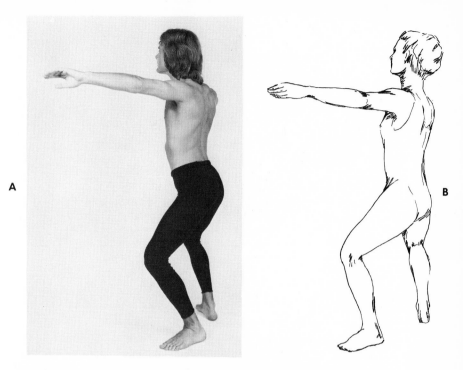

Fig. 3-4. Landing from a second position jump. **A,** Incorrect positioning. The shock of landing is not distributed equally along the entire length of the dancer's body. Knees are not positioned over the center of the feet, lower back is arched, and head is thrust forward. **B,** Correct positioning. Stress of landing is less when the head, trunk, and legs are correctly aligned. Shock is transmitted equally along the outer length of the spine, starting at the feet and ending at the base of the head.

effects. All human beings have variations in their basic constitutional strengths based on their inherited physiques. Just as some individuals inherit organic susceptibilities to various diseases such as heart disease and visual problems, individuals inherit peculiarities in body structure that may or may not decrease their ability to withstand physical stresses. Often the dancer's awareness of a potential physical weakness can be dealt with positively by employing better conditioning methods and avoiding activities that may aggravate the problem or prolong it.

Fatigue is a factor that the dancer fights continually. The most likely times for injuries to occur are in the early stages of a new dance experience when the body is not adequately trained and in the very late periods of a dance session when chronic physical and mental tiredness make the dancer extremely vulnerable to injury. Elimination of fatigue is best accomplished by a constant

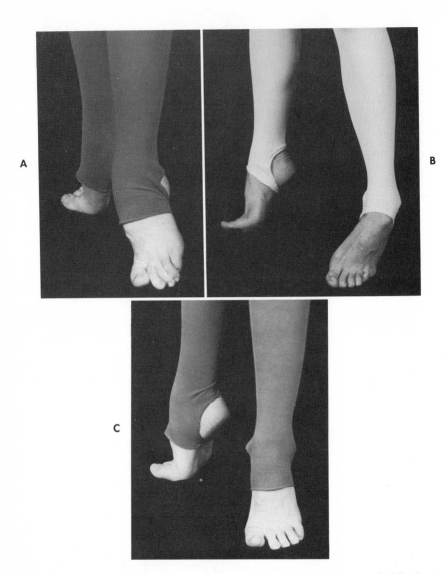

Fig. 3-5. Foot and ankle placement. **A,** Incorrect positioning with sickling in. Sickling in, or eversion and pronation of the foot and ankle, causes strain on the longitudinal arch and the great toe and tends to roll the heel outward. **B,** Incorrect positioning with sickling out. Inversion, or a rolling inward of the foot, places great strain on the outer tendons and ligaments of the foot and ankle. **C,** Correct positioning with good lower limb placement. The toes are, for the most part, straight and flat on the supporting surface as well as properly aligned with the forefoot. The forefoot forms a straight line to the midfoot, the back of the foot, and the lower leg.

Fig. 3-6. Sitting stretch in second position. **A,** Incorrect positioning. Dancer is rolling the hip and thigh inward and rounding the upper back. In this faulty position, strain may occur to the groin and inner thigh. **B,** Correct positioning. Injury is not likely because the legs and feet are in a straight line with the pelvis, resulting in equal contraction of the internal and external muscles of the hip. Extending the spine maintains the pelvis in good alignment with both the trunk and thighs.

program of training to ensure an optimum level of strength and flexibility combined with muscular and cardiovascular endurance.

Dancers must continually adjust to their environment. The dance environments of the stage and studio present tremendous demands on the body and emotional system in an effort to adjust to variations in area, size, and surface resistance. Stage surfaces can accentuate the problems of the dancer's fatigue. Ideally the dance surface should have resiliency, yielding to the force of the dancer's body. Dancing on a rigid nonyielding surface overtaxes tendons, joints, and bones and may eventually lead to acute or chronic pathologic conditions.

part three

Injury prevention

Part 3 presents an overview of the many factors that are related to the prevention of injuries occurring in dance.

chapter four

Conditioning

Proper conditioning is vital for the dancer. In order for anyone to efficiently execute a motor task there must be adequate strength, flexibility, and endurance.

Strength

Strength is the most important physiological factor in the prevention of dance injuries. It is defined as the capacity of the individual to exert a muscle contraction or force against a resistance. When muscles are regularly exercised, important physiological changes take place as well as an increase in muscle girth or size. However, for a muscle to develop size and strength it must be stressed by progressive overloading.

For example, an individual can engage in an increased number of repetitions of a particular movement and produce strength up to a point. However, this type of exercise will increase the dancer's ability to sustain a specific movement rather than increase strength. Other means of overloading can be applied by gradually increasing a resistance to a specific muscle or group of muscles. For the best results in overloading, a muscle exercise should be executed in a scientific manner. For example, it has been found that strength can be effectively gained when a three-quarter maximum resistance is used in an overload program.

Strength may be identified in two specific areas. One is the ability of the individual to overcome resistance through a complete range of movement, which is called isotonic strength. A second type of strength (used very little in dance) is isometric strength, which is the ability to apply resistance against an immovable force.

Because strength in general allows the dancer to move freely and handle the body efficiently, it also plays an extremely important role in the prevention of injury. However, for strength to be most effective it must be properly balanced between the agonist and antagonist muscles. Therefore a dancer concerned with injury prevention should be concerned with all-around muscle development, avoiding overdeveloping strength of specific muscle groups.

Flexibility

Flexibility is one of the dancer's most important concerns. Flexibility can be defined in many different ways, but in essence it is the amplitude of joint movement or the extent to which a limb can be extended and flexed. There are many causes for a decrease or increase of flexibility: anatomical, physiological, or even emotional. The human body varies greatly in its ability to engage in a broad spectrum of movement. One such variation is in the dancer's joint structure. A person who has a heavy skeletal formation may not be able to engage in a full range of movement activity as can an individual who has a lighter or more delicate design. On the other hand, joints may differ according to their ligamentous organization. A joint that is heavily bound by ligaments may be more restricted than a lightly supported joint. Bulky musculature and tight, unyielding tendons can also restrict the range of movement. Since one muscle is relaxed while an opposing muscle is contracting, the dancer can consciously "let go" of a part. This is commonly called reciprocal coordination. Although most restricted movements of joints and limbs are of an anatomical or physiological origin, a person's mental and emotional characteristics have a great deal to do with his ability to relax. The tense individual who appears restricted and withdrawn because of painful emotions often reflects these feelings in a rigid and unyielding body.

One must be reminded that posture affects the pliability and extensibility of the body's musculature. When considering flexibility, one must also be reminded that the habitual positions that one takes in life can alter joint range of motion. The more sendentary people are, the less able they are to perform a variety of movements. Very active persons, on the other hand, who engage in a variety of different activities throughout the day will usually be more flexible than their less active peers.

Increasing joint range of movement

In recent years there has been much discussion as to the best method to increase and maintain flexibility. The major groups involved in this controversy on stretching have been the proponents of ballistic (bouncing) stretching and those individuals who believe that static or gradually increased stretching is the best approach.

Ballistic stretching can be defined as that stretch in which the performer progressively bounces to increase the length of a particular muscle group. Uncontrolled ballistic stretching is dangerous because the performer often allows the body part to be overstretched. The safest of the ballistic stretches is the controlled ballistic stretch, in which the participant pulls the body into the stretch in a controlled manner. The static or gradual stretch is different from the ballistic type; the performer takes the desired position of stretch and pulls the body to the point where it can no longer go, and then gradually tries to pull past this position for 30 seconds to 1 minute. The performer is instructed to bring the stretched part to a point of discomfort and to gradually attempt to go beyond this point. While at the resistance point, the performer should force all air from the lungs, allowing the stretch to be increased, sometimes as much as 2 to 6 inches. Studies have shown that the controlled ballistic and the static stretch are equally effective in increasing range of movement; however, ballistic stretch tends to aggravate muscle tissue, and small muscle tears and spasms may occur, discouraging the performer in attempts to further engage in activity. Static stretching tends to decrease the tendency toward muscle spasm and muscle soreness in the very early stages of activity. Consequently, gradual stretch is preferred, particularly in the very early stages of a conditioning program.

In essence, stretching exercises are most effective when executed slowly and deliberately rather than with bouncing or jerking movements. Ballistic movements tend to stimulate the stretch reflex and, in some cases, overly tense muscles instead of producing relaxation, making them vulnerable to spasms and tearing. Selected stretches for the major areas of the body are shown in Figs. 4-1 to 4-8.

A third technique of stretching is fast becoming popular among dancers and athletes alike. This technique uses the concept of muscle relaxation through facilitation of the proprioceptors.* This approach utilizes the natural physiological fact that a muscle contraction is normally followed by relaxation of the opposite antagonist muscle. The purpose of the facilitation method is to

---

*For more information see Knott, M., and Voss, D. E.: Proprioceptive neuromuscular facilitation, ed. 2, New York, 1968, Harper & Row, Publishers.

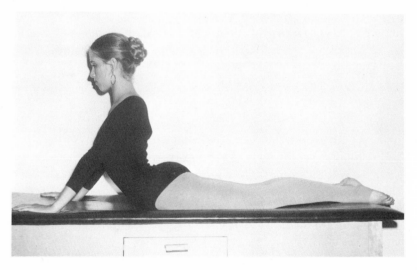

Fig. 4-1. Trunk stretch. Dancer extends arms and maintains a flat pelvis. *This stretch should be avoided by dancers with low back problems.*

Fig. 4-2. Shoulder, abdomen, and hip stretch. Grasping the ankles, the dancer pulls until a stretch is felt in the frontal aspect of the trunk and hips.

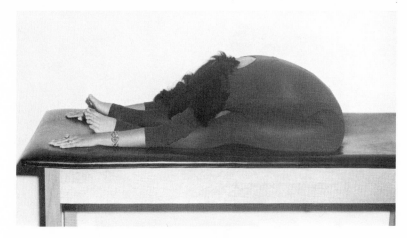

Fig. 4-3. Hamstring and low back stretch. The dancer extends the legs fully with the ankles relaxed, grasps the feet, and pulls the trunk downward.

Fig. 4-4. Upper and lower back stretch. Raising the legs over the head, the dancer touches toes to the floor.

purposefully stimulate the neural mechanisms of contraction and relaxation. One method applicable to dance is to forcibly contract one set of muscles against a resistance and then immediately begin a gradual stretch of the opposing muscle group. For example, the dancer extends the lower leg several times against a resistance such as a fellow dancer's hand or a wall (contracting the quadriceps muscles as much as possible), and immediately follows with a gradual (static)

Fig. 4-5. Trunk rotator stretch. Pressing against a bent knee with the arm, the dancer rotates the trunk in the opposite direction, then repeats in the other direction.

Fig. 4-6. Calf stretch. Standing at arm's length from the barre, the body is inclined forward. The leg to be stretched is extended with the foot flat on the floor.

Fig. 4-7. Front of leg stretch. Placing the toes on a rolled-up towel, the dancer sits on feet.

Fig. 4-8. Shoulder stretch. The dancer grasps the hands behind the back, one from above, the other from below. The hand positions are then reversed.

stretch of the hamstring group. This same procedure could be applied in any body area. If the application of a resistance is impractical or difficult, the dancer can still facilitate stimulation by three or four quick isotonic (no resistance) contractions of the opposing muscle followed by a stretch.

Managing muscular soreness and stiffness

There are many theories as to why active persons develop muscle soreness following physical activity. A common belief is that soreness develops in muscles as a result of minute muscle spasms and perhaps even small muscle tears. This causes a mild inflammation in the muscle with resultant pain caused by the pressure of swelling on pain receptors. Soreness often follows unaccustomed physical activity. Stiffness is associated with the same circumstances as muscle soreness; however, it is not as apparent and is probably the result of metabolites that have collected within the muscle tissue. In cases of both muscular soreness and stiffness the dancer complains of a decrease in muscle tissue extensibility and limb flexibility.

A proved method to help overcome muscle soreness and stiffness is to follow a program of gradual stretching at the beginning of an intense exercise period and to follow up with the same stretching regime at the end of the class. Stretching at the end of class helps to decrease muscle spasms, thereby decreasing abnormal pressure on nerve endings. This procedure is best followed for about 2 weeks in a new class. After the 2-week period has passed, the body has become accustomed to using different muscles and may require only a gradual stretching regime at the beginning of the class session or actual performance.

In conclusion, flexibility is specific for the types of activities that are engaged in, with each person having his own flexibility characteristics. It is important that the dancer eliminate the possibility of sudden strain or twist by being as flexible as possible. However, joint range of movement should not be developed at the expense of a balance of strength. The dancer who acquires a high level of muscle extensibility is able to use the body effectively and is often able to withstand the injury-producing stresses that are inherent in dance. Flexibility can also help to reduce the shock to the body that comes from unyielding floor or stage surfaces. Muscles that have good extensibility respond to a twist or a sudden jerk without spasm or tissue tension.

Endurance

Endurance is the staying power of the body and is divided into two components: muscle endurance and cardiovascular endurance. Muscle endurance is the ability of the dancer to sustain many muscle contractions over a given period of time. Muscle endurance cannot be separated from muscle strength because it is part of a continuum. The dancer's muscle endurance is of the utmost importance to sustain a high quality of movement for a long period of time. Because dancing can be one of the most grueling of endeavors, requiring many hours dedicated to practice, the efficiency of the heart and lungs must not be discounted. The efficiency of the cardiovascular system is inseparable from the other components of the dancer's physical fitness. The body cannot be used effectively as a tool for creative expression without all physical fitness factors being at the highest level possible. The ability to effectively deliver oxygen to the muscle tissue over a long period of time demands a strong and efficient cardiorespiratory system. In order to produce an oxygen delivery system that is efficient and able to withstand the rigors of long hours of physical activity, the heart muscle must be strong. In the well-conditioned heart muscle, each contraction places a greater than average volume of blood into the general circulation. As the heart becomes trained, it also becomes slower in beats per minute. Training sometimes reduces the pulse rate as much as 10 to 20 beats per minute as efficiency increases. The well-conditioned heart also returns to its normal beat much more quickly than the poorly conditioned heart and recuperates more quickly from physical fatigue. Because of the better transportation of oxygen to all the body's tissue, the metabolites are more quickly removed. The trained respiratory system is able to handle oxygen more efficiently; consequently, there is an increased use of oxygen. The trained dancer with an efficient cardiovascular system is able to endure a high level of physical performance for a long period of time without the distress of physical fatigue.

To improve efficiency of the heart and lungs, the overload principle must be employed as it is in improving strength. Cardiovascular endurance, therefore, can be increased by the dancer forcing the body to engage in activity over a long period of time, gradually increasing the rate and intensity of training. The serious dancer should be extremely concerned with the efficiency of the cardiovascular system. While not participating in dance, the dancer should engage in different types of sustained activity such as bicycling, jogging, and to a lesser degree, even swimming. A good subjective indication of increasing cardiovascular fitness is a pulse rate that becomes slower as training progresses.

Warming up and warming down

The concept of warm-up has been debated for many decades; it is still considered unnecessary by some authorities but, with the vast majority of professionals in exercise physiology, we consider a warm-up as a necessary prelude to dancing. However, research has found that the use of such warm-up procedures as massage, use of analgesic balms, and hot showers have little effect on performance. Most professionals in the areas of physical activity agree that a good warm-up is necessary in order to prevent strains and muscle tears that arise from sudden overstretching of the musculotendinous unit. There is, however, vast disagreement as to how much and what type of activity is necessary to adequately warm up the performer. In general the primary purpose of a warm-up before vigorous physical activity is to raise the deep temperatures within the body and to elongate contracted ligaments and fascia as well as musculature. If these factors are taken into consideration, the body is then able to withstand the various rigors of intensive physical activity. Research has also shown that proper warm-up increases the speed of nerve impulse transmission. It must be concluded that warm-up is a necessary procedure in preparation for vigorous physical activity.

A proper warm-up, depending on the activity to be engaged in and the vigor that the activity demands, should last from 10 to 20 or even 30 minutes, until a sweat has been broken and the body has been fully stretched. Warm-up procedures should range from general to specific movements. The dancer should first be concerned with increasing the heart rate and gradually increasing the deep temperatures of the body. This can be accomplished by easy running or prancing in place or around the studio, followed by light general movement of all the joints. When perspiration has broken out on the skin and a feeling of body warmth is experienced, the dancer should then proceed with a stretching routine including either the gradual stretch or facilitative techniques or both. Following the stretch phase, the dancer should be concerned with "stylized" warming up, involving the primary movements or combinations that will be utilized in the dance to be performed. It is extremely important in terms of injury prevention that the dancer finish the warm-up session with movements from the dance that will be performed. Following this warm-up approach, the body is in a state of readiness: there is an increase in temperature, blood sugar, and adrenaline, and joints are unencumbered in preparation for vigorous activity. Also, it must be concluded that the older performer needs a longer warm-up period than the younger dancer.

Following vigorous dancing, the dancer should allow the body to gradually warm down. Circulation should be permitted to slow down gradually with the heart rate returning to the preexercise level. It is extremely harmful to stop activity while the heart is pumping vigorously. In this situation body fluids tend to pool in the lower limbs, causing extreme discomfort and soreness. Rather than stopping suddenly, the dancer should continue to move around for 3 to 5 minutes following activity until the heart rate and breathing have returned to normal. At the conclusion of a class or a performance when the heart rate has returned to normal, the dancer should then engage in a general stretching routine to overcome the small muscle spasms that have arisen.

It is not the intent of this book to go into full detail about the areas of conditioning. If the reader is interested in further information, it is suggested he read books dedicated to exercise physiology and athletic training, as these are also applicable to dance.*

---

*For example, see Klafs, C. E., and Arnheim, D. D.: Modern principles of athletic training, ed. 3, St. Louis, 1973, The C. V. Mosby Co.

chapter five

Nutrition

When one considers all the factors that help to prevent injury, nutrition must be considered as one of the most important. Because of the extreme demands the dancer places on the body, what is ingested into the body must be of the highest quality. Like the athlete, the dancer is prone to food fallacies and fads in an attempt to improve performance. Such beliefs and practices often only serve to hamper performance and, in many cases where there is injury, delay the healing process.

Food categories

In order for dancers to engage in strenuous activities their bodies must have sufficient nutrients to properly supply the working muscles. Good nutrition involves the daily intake of six primary substances in balanced amounts to provide normal organic function. These substances are carbohydrates, fats, proteins, minerals, vitamins, and water. Each must be present in the body in a particular percentage. Carbohydrates should constitute about 50% to 55% of the diet; fats, from 35% to 40%; and proteins, from 10% to 15%; together with proper amounts of vitamins, minerals, and water.

Carbohydrates, which are made up of the elements of carbon, hydrogen, and oxygen, are found in such food substances as starches, sugars, breadstuffs, potatoes, and rice, and when ingested into the body they become readily available as energy sources. Carbohydrates are stored in the liver as glycogen and serve to overcome the sense of fatigue when there is a sugar depletion in the blood. Fat, although similar in composition to carbohydrates, is present in a more complex form. Fats are usually stored in the body as a reserve source of fuel and energy. Because of the difficulty of utilization, fat is not considered as ready a source of energy as carbohydrates.

Protein is mainly utilized by the body for tissue building, repair of tissue, and regulation of body functions. Contrary to current thought among many dancers, more than 10% to 15% of protein in the diet does not add markedly to strength or endurance. Only when there is an extremely heavy strength overload program does the body utilize a greater percentage of protein.

The organic compounds known as vitamins do not function as energy producers nor do they build tissue, although they do catalyze other organic compounds to produce energy and build tissue. At this time, approximately 26 vitamins have been identified. Of this list, vitamins A, B complex, and D are the most well known. Vitamin A is essential for cellular growth and assists in combating bacterial infection. Deficiency in vitamin A also produces night blindness. Vitamin A is found in red or orange foods such as carrots and in leafy vegetables. Vitamin B complex (B_1, B_2, and B_{12}) is essential for the function of enzymes, utilization of carbohydrates, normal growth, and basic organic functions. Because vitamin B complex has a water base, it is not stored in the body and must be taken in the diet on a daily basis. It can be found in liver, brewer's yeast, fruits, and vegetables. Vitamin C is probably the most unstable of all vitamins and is also water soluble. Vitamin C is essential for the formation of the material that binds cells together. It is essential in the healing of injuries such as often occur to soft tissue. It also assists the dancer in combating stress. Vitamin C is found in citrus fruits and many vegetables such as cabbage. Vitamin D, like vitamin A, has an oil base and is stored in the body. An overdose of either one of these vitamins may be toxic. Vitamin D is essential for bone growth and cellular function. It is found commonly in milk, cod liver oil, and fish.

Of all the nutritional substances, minerals are probably the least understood. However, as a common food element they are essential for proper functioning of the body and in the maintenance of life. Without the proper balance of such minerals as calcium, sodium, potassium, and magnesium, normal cellular function is impossible. Other trace elements such as cobalt, copper, iodine, manganese, and iron are essential for various cellular functions. The physically active person will experience many symptoms when there are decreased amounts of minerals in the body, such as muscle cramping, fatigue, and slow recovery from the effects of physical activity. A balanced diet, which contains an abundance of water and a variety of vegetables, should provide the requirements of minerals to the body. Salt or sodium chloride supplementation will be discussed in more detail in the section on heat stress (p. 71).

If the dancer takes in the basic food groups in the correct proportions each day, the nutrients that are required for a vigorous and physically active life will be provided. The major foods necessary for efficient physical activity are milk, meats, vegetables and fruits, and breads and cereals. The dancer should avoid food fads and strive for a balanced approach to eating.*

Food supplementation

There is a current tendency among physically active people, particularly those individuals who are continuously dieting, to supplement their diets with vitamin and protein pills. For the most part, this practice does little good and is probably a waste of money. A balanced diet will provide all that an active person requires. However, the individual who eats irregularly and realizes that his diet is not complete should take supplements containing the minimum daily requirements of vitamins and minerals. High-potency vitamins should be avoided at all times. Intake of potentially toxic vitamins such as A and D should be avoided. Increasing vitamin dosage in an unscientific manner may disrupt the delicate organic chemical balance of the body.

Food routines

Dancers are concerned about what types of food to consume before a performance. In actuality, pre-dance performance nutrition must vary with the dancer. However, research does indicate that gastric distress due to nervousness can be alleviated to a great extent if the meal is eaten approximately 4 hours before the performance. This allows the food to be digested out of the stomach and into the intestinal tract. This is not to say, however, that the dancer should go into a performance hungry. Hunger may adversely affect performance. It is suggested that those who feel hunger pangs drink a 4- to 6-ounce can of liquid diet drink. Intake of a diet drink will satiate hunger pangs and at the same time provide some bulk for the stomach without causing distress or gas. The food that

---

*Further nutritional information can be obtained from Bogert, J., Briggs, G. M., and Calloway, D. H.: Nutrition and physical fitness, ed. 9, Philadelphia, 1973, W. B. Saunders Co.

should be eaten during the 4-hour period before performance usually varies with the individual taste and life-style of the dancer. However, it is suggested that food be selected from those that are easily digested. The approximate time required for foods to leave the stomach are as follows: beef, 3 hours; lamb or pork, 3¼ hours; vegetables and fruits, 2¾ hours; desserts such as cake, 3½ hours; cereal products, 2½ hours; and milk 2¾ hours. A dancer who sits down to a meal 4 hours before a vigorous performance has most of the food out of his stomach before activity commences. In general the dancer should eat foods that do not cause gastric distress. Special foods eaten with the intent to create more energy or strength will have little effect on the dancer just prior to a performance. If the dancer plans to expend a great deal of energy, foods high in carbohydrates should be eaten for 3 or 4 days before the performance. Glycogen from foods such as pasta, cereals, breads, and rice will be stored in the liver and become readily available as energy for the performance.

Weight control

Weight control is one of the most difficult problems the dancer has to face. The problem of losing weight often causes the dancer to engage in fads and harmful diet practices that result in less than optimum functioning of the entire body. The dancer must practice an intelligent approach to weight control, avoiding fads and eating a balanced diet. Simply said, overweight is caused by taking in more energy in food than the body expends in activity. To lose weight the dancer must reverse this process. However, rapid weight loss in a short period of time may be harmful; therefore every effort must be expended to lose weight over a long period of time. No more than 2 or 3 pounds should be lost in a week. Fat that is taken off gradually has a tendency to stay off, while weight that is lost rapidly tends to be replaced rapidly. The crash diet serves only to increase susceptibility to the common cold and often, because of weakness, makes the dancer susceptible to traumatic injuries. Dehydration should be avoided at all costs because the practice of eliminating water from the diet combined with profuse sweating depletes the body of minerals and may cause muscle cramping and muscle tears. The best way to achieve weight reduction is to eat a balanced diet but decrease the number of calories ingested during the day. If the dancer who has a normal metabolism decreases the normal daily calorie intake by 500 calories, ½ pound of fat can be lost about every 3 days.

Because of variations in body build, particularly among female dancers, many desire to spot reduce certain areas of the body such as the hips and thighs. Research has shown that spot reduction is extremely unlikely by the sweat method. The best means of spot reduction is by an exercise program involving many repetitions in a full range of movement and involving numerous muscle contractions in the specific area; for example, for reducing the hips, the dancer lies on one side and executes 20 to 30 leg lifts, bringing the side of the leg as high as possible and down. This method discourages heavy muscle development and encourages longer muscle fibers to develop, as well as reducing the amount of fat in the area. Weight gain, on the other hand, is best attained by increasing the amount of food intake beyond the daily expenditure. However, the intake of an overabundance of fatty foods should be discouraged.

The method of using height and weight charts for determining optimum body weight must be considered inaccurate and too general for the dancer to follow. The best means of determining the amount of fat distribution in the body is by use of skinfold calipers (Fig. 5-1). The most characteristic fat area for both men and women is the triceps area (back of arm). Body fat ideally should not exceed 7% to 8% of the total body weight. Other areas of fat accumulation are the abdominal area, the buttocks, and the superiliac and subscapular regions.

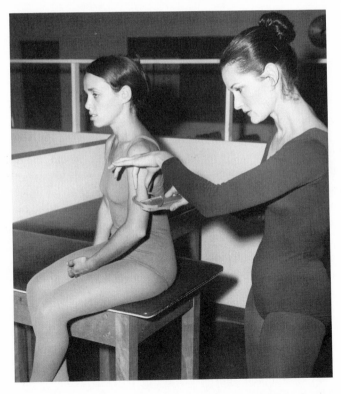

Fig. 5-1. Determining body fat by the skinfold caliper method.

Skinfold measurements at these sites ideally should not exceed 8 to 10 mm. In other words, any area in which the dancer can pinch ½ to ¾ inch may be considered to contain too much fat.

Heat stress

The dancer's reaction to high temperatures is very important. Hot stage lights and poor air circulation can contribute to extreme temperatures and cause serious physiological problems for the dancer. Often adding to these heat conditions are costumes that keep heat in, not allowing perspiration to evaporate and cool the body. The dancer can lose from 2 to 6 pounds or more of water in one performance. When the temperature exceeds 89° F., the only means by which the body can dissipate heat is through perspiration. If the humidity is also high, evaporation is restricted and sweating may not adequately cool the body, causing the internal temperature of the dancer to rise. The first indication of adverse effects of heat are muscle cramps that result from excess perspiration and the elimination of salt and various other minerals from the body. Excessive mineral loss increases motor nerve excitability and results in cramping. Of course, when the dancer continues to work on cramped muscles, the results are muscle pulls and tears. If a dancer insists on continuing to dance while experiencing high temperatures and humidity, a condition called heat exhaustion can occur.

Heat exhaustion is caused by a depletion of body fluids and results in a general letdown of the body processes such as commonly seen in shock. The dancer complains of extreme fatigue and chills and has cold beads of sweat on the forehead, under the eyes, and on the upper lip. The pulse is rapid and weak. Under such circumstances as heat exhaustion the dancer should be treated symptomatically. If there is a sense of coldness, the dancer should be covered and, of course, taken out of the adverse environment and allowed to rest. If the dancer continues to exercise while experiencing heat exhaustion, a very serious complication known as heat stroke could arise.

Heat stroke presents a different set of symptoms than heat exhaustion. The dancer may collapse, the skin is dry, the heart rate is very slow and weak, the face may be red, and breathing comes in labored gasps. Under these circumstances, immediate medical attention must be sought. The dancer must be cooled down immediately because the internal temperature may go as high as 106° F., and death could follow. Immediate care should include removing tight clothing and placing cold, wet cloths on the back of the neck, stomach, and legs and under the arms, followed by rapid fanning to drop the temperatures as fast as possible. If ice is available, it is preferable to cold, wet cloths.

The reader should note that most individuals can become acclimatized to extremely adverse environmental conditions, including high temperatures and humidity; however, acclimatization takes from 1 to 2 weeks. Under adverse climatic conditions the dancer should practice during the coolest time of day and in the beginning should not work more than ½ hour at a time. Fluid should be taken when needed, and the dancer should be cognizant of the amount of weight loss that occurs following each practice session. It has been determined that 3% or more weight loss during one exercise period demands special concern. A 10-grain salt tablet should be taken for every ½ pound of body weight lost. This is the only time that salt tablets should be taken. This is particularly true in the very early stages of conditioning. Other factors such as vitamin C supplementation may help the dancer withstand the stresses that high humidity and temperatures produce. The dancer should never attempt a weight reduction program during this type of climatic situation.

Energy aids

The term "ergogenic" means work-producing and is used in the context of physical activity to describe agents taken into the body for the express purpose of improving performance. Besides substances taken into the system, an ergogen can also be a motivational technique designed to improve performance. In today's society it is becoming commonplace to take various substances to increase performance or to delay the onset of the feeling of fatigue. Some dancers (although not many) attempt to improve their performances by questionable practices. These include the overuse of stimulants such as coffee and tea, amphetamines such as Benzedrine or Dexedrine, or so-called "downers" such as alcohol and barbiturates. Amphetamines (pep pills) function as powerful stimulants to the central nervous system, which increases the heart rate and blood pressure and produces a general feeling of alertness and well-being. Amphetamines are most often used by persons engaged in physical activity to overcome the feeling of fatigue. Some individuals react adversely to amphetamines; they may produce dizziness, depression, hallucinations, and poor judgment. Users of pep pills often believe a performance is going well when in actuality it is mediocre or even poor.

Oxygen is another type of ergogenic aid used for overcoming the distress of fatigue. This practice has no foundation in research. To the contrary, oxygen is of little value because in conditions of extreme physical activity the red blood cells are as saturated with oxygen as they can possibly be. The introduction of additional oxygen has little value for the performer. Another means of bettering performance that has been used by dancers is hypnosis. Research has shown that hypnosis can aid in strength and endurance to some extent. Further research must be conducted on how hypnosis affects performance, but at this time the value seems to be that it tends to release psychological inhibiting factors. In doing so the performer is able to expend a greater amount of energy over a longer period of time.

Sugar is a substance that, if properly used, can improve endurance. Table sugar, dextrose, glucose, and honey are all forms of food and may eventually provide energy for muscle contraction. However, nutritionists indicate that the ingestion of these substances has little effect on activities of short duration. In cases where prolonged muscular contraction is to be engaged in, as in a dance class or performance, the practice of ingesting increased amounts of sugar may be beneficial. Sugar taken orally by itself tends to draw fluid from the body into the gastrointestinal tract and somewhat dehydrates the individual. A better way of bringing sugar to the body is through highly sweetened tea with lemon, which helps to eliminate the dehydrating effect of sugar alone.

chapter six

Psychological factors

The psychological aspect of injury prevention is as important to the dancer as proper conditioning and nutrition. Dancers, like all people, have varying personalities and react to stress in unique ways. What sets the dancer off as unique from other individuals is that he is both an athlete and an artist seeking perfection in movement. The dancer can have peculiarities that may enhance or detract from neuromuscular control. There is no artistic endeavor that places the mental and emotional demands on the individual that dance does. Consequently, psychological maturity is as important to the dancer as physical conditioning. The extent to which the dancer can withstand the psychological stresses imposed by the dance environment is determined by the dancer's total emotional development and life-style, both past and present.

Accident-proneness

The accident-prone dancer is one who experiences more injuries than would be considered normal. There are two times at which accidents normally have a higher incidence: at the beginning of a semester or a new series of dance classes and at the end of a series of classes. One can speculate that the reason for an increased number of injuries at the beginning may be the dancer's attempts to execute techniques beyond the present ability level or inadequate conditioning.

At the end of a particular set of classes, injuries may be due to fatigue, both mental and physical, in which the dancer fails to be alert enough to avoid dangerous situations.

In the dance field, as in athletics, three types of psychological accident-proneness can be identified.* An accident-prone dancer can be categorized as (1) the actually injured performer, (2) the performer with imagined injuries, or (3) the malingerer. The actually injured accident-prone dancer is characterized by the fact that the injuries can be identified by the presence of specific pathologic conditions. It can be speculated that the cause of the actually injured type may be a subconscious desire for punishment through a physical injury. The dancer may work to the point that the body actually breaks down or may continually become involved in dangerous situations in which injury is imminent. On the other hand, individuals whose injuries are imagined are those who feel pain but under close medical scrutiny reveal no pathologic condition. These individuals are much like a fine clock wound too tightly. They set their sights too high and are unable to attain their aspirations; consequently, they escape through imagined injury. Imagined injuries are often seen in dancers just before participating in a new work or just before going on the stage. This reaction to fear is normal. However, it is the individual who year after year has imagined injuries that detract from his normal functioning that may be considered unsound. The malingerer is the individual who purposely falsifies an injury to escape work or a personally uncomfortable situation. This individual must be classed as psychologically immature and unable to face life's problems in an adult manner.

It is not the intent of this manual to discuss in detail the psychological factors that make up the complex matrix of human behavior. However, it is important to provide the reader with these more apparent psychological factors that make a dancer more or less prone to injury. It is always well to understand why a dancer chooses dance as a field for self-expression. Understanding why dancers dance can also give an indication of why a particular dancer is accident-prone and another is seldom bothered by any physical disturbance.

Tension and dance

When considering injuries associated with psychogenic factors, one must consider muscular tension as a major cause in the dance field. Tension is defined as increased muscular contraction as a result of some emotional state or

---

*For more information see Olgilvie, B. C., and Tutko, T. A.: Problem athletes and how to handle them, London, 1966, Pelham Books, Ltd.

muscular work. Nervous tension is a syndrome that is characteristic of the so-called "fast way of life" of our times. It is associated with anxiety that comes from an undefined worry or fear. An overanxious dancer can have an extremely high level of unneeded muscular tension. The person who is anxious outwardly may be less flexible and less able to smoothly coordinate muscles. Organically he may have an increased heart rate and blood pressure. The tense dancer is extremely susceptible to injury and because of this increased muscular excitability may overrespond to painful conditions. The ability to eliminate muscular tension by consciously "letting go" is very important to all dancers. Dancers who can relax at will can increase their mental and physical efficiency.

Respiration, circulation, and coordination are positively affected when relaxation is controlled. For example, there is a more efficient exchange of oxygen and carbon dioxide when the muscles of inspiration and expiration are without tension. Blood can circulate unimpeded when the blood vessels are not overly constricted by the pressure of the musculature, and the dancer is more easily able to engage in differential relaxation, which allows smooth coordination of the agonist and antagonist muscles.

Although anxiety must be controlled when the dancer is engaged in activity over a long period of time, preperformance jitters or tension is considered normal. Preperformance tension is a normal part of getting ready for activity. Even the most experienced dancer goes through this syndrome, sometimes to the point of nausea and vomiting. However, once on stage the professional soon forgets the fear and performs effectively. The preperformance jitters are nature's way of preparing the dancer for maximal expenditure of energy. The primary glands that bring about the readiness state are the adrenal glands, which secrete the hormone adrenaline as part of their function. Adrenaline is released into the bloodstream to speed up circulation and respiration and to assist in bringing fuel to the muscles. It also increases the removal of metabolites and other waste products from the muscles. Associated with the readiness state may be feelings of anxiety, breathlessness, butterflies in the stomach to the point of nausea, dry mouth, and an increase in the action of the bowels. All of these are normal responses to getting ready to perform. Without this reaction to the forthcoming performance, the dancer may in fact be put in a situation where an injury might be incurred. The readiness condition places the body in a state that makes injury less likely.

Staleness

Staleness is a period of physical and emotional letdown that usually follows a long period of intense physical exertion and is associated with an inability to relax and rest comfortably. It may also be associated with a loss of appetite, digestive problems, weight loss, and a general feeling of lethargy. Staleness is common among dancers during periods where there has been an extremely long season of practice without letup or after a very discouraging tour in which expectations have not been met. In such cases the dancer feels fatigue and extreme letdown with an inability to get emotionally "up" for the next performance. Because staleness is primarily a mental state rather than a physical problem, it is best handled by reasoning or by a change of pace. When staleness is apparent, the dancer should completely change the environment and do something entirely different. If this is not possible, the dancer should at least attempt to change the pace by varying a basic routine. Sometimes just a little praise from an important person can make all the difference in the world to a dancer who is becoming stale. It must be brought out that the dancer who is in a stale period is extremely susceptible to injury and that injury situations must be avoided at all cost. Accident-proneness is very probable during this emotionally low period.

part four

Principles of injury care

Part 4 provides important information necessary to intelligently evaluate injuries arising from dance. It also gives a commonsense rationale in applying immediate and follow-up care for the most prevalent conditions occurring in dance.

chapter seven

Evaluating injuries

It is extremely important that all persons connected with dance have the ability to intelligently recognize and evaluate the seriousness of an injury. Too often, because of the press of time and circumstances, an injury is neglected to the extent that it becomes chronic, causing the dancer many hours of unnecessary recovery time. It is the intent of this chapter to help the reader to understand the nature of traumatic injuries.

Traumatic dance injuries are either internal or external. External injuries are the exposed type and include such skin conditions as abrasions, lacerations, and incisions. Internal injuries are for the most part unexposed, constituting conditions of the musculoskeletal system such as contusions, strains, sprains, dislocations, and fractures.

The inflammatory process is involved in both exposed and unexposed injuries. Inflammation occurs when the body tissues are irritated and react with redness, heat, swelling, pain, and in some cases, cellular malfunctioning. Whatever the irritant may be, traumatic, chemical, thermal, or pathogenic, cellular disruption results in metabolic changes that produce the inflammatory process. In general, inflammation is a protective process designed to repair and heal the body.

When an injury occurs, a vascular reaction brings about a fluid imbalance at the injury site. At the moment trauma occurs, blood vessels and capillaries constrict at the point of tissue insult, emptying the area of blood for a short period of time. Following constriction, capillary dilation occurs, which allows a flood of blood and serum into the area of injury. This fluid causes pressure on exposed nerve endings, resulting in pain. Immediately at the time of tissue insult, hormones direct white blood cells to the area to begin the process of removing debris from the area. At the same time, repair and healing begin, with the injured site becoming organized into a blood clot that later becomes a fibrous scar.

Ideally healing should take place with as little scarring as possible. Scar tissue is basically an inferior tissue and is susceptible to repeated injuries. Two types of injury healing occur: primary healing, or healing by first intention, and secondary healing, or healing by second intention. Primary healing is the type of healing that produces little scarring because the edges of the wound are closely approximated. Secondary healing is the type of healing that occurs where there has been a great deal of tissue damage, and the edges of the wound are gapped. Most traumatic injuries of the body heal by secondary intention.

Three procedures are usually followed in the initial stages of caring for an injury to assist nature in the inflammation process and repair. These three procedures are compression, cold, and elevation. Outside compression of the injury helps to prevent the accumulation of fluids. Immediate cold to an area constricts superficial blood vessels and helps to keep fluid accumulation (edema) and swelling under control. Elevation is also designed to slow down circulation at the injured site. Immediate care properly applied does not reduce the pathologic damage actually present in the area, but compression, cold, and elevation help make the injured area more amenable to follow-up therapy. These procedures are discussed in more detail in Chapter 8.

Dancers are susceptible to acute musculoskeletal problems caused by forces that overly stretch or compress selected tissues of the body. A force that causes a sudden insult to the body produces an acute injury that, if managed properly, should be of short duration. Early management includes pressure from an Ace bandage, cold in the form of ice packs or cold water immersion, elevation, and in some cases complete immobilization of the part (Chapter 8).

Acute unexposed injuries

There is a high incidence of *contusions* among active persons. A contusion is a bruise resulting in variable degrees of pathologic damage, depending on the force of the blow and its body locality. A contusion can crush tissue, disrupting the continuity of capillaries and causing swelling as well as occasionally resulting in a hematoma, or blood tumor. A hematoma can be described as the localization of the bleeding site into a clot surrounded by a connective tissue membrane. A severe contusion can cause extreme pain, swelling, and in some cases a temporary paralysis caused by the combined pressure of the swelling and muscle spasm on nerves.

Muscle strain, which is caused by an overstretching of the musculotendinous unit (the entire muscle and the tendons), is the most common problem that the dancer must face. It can range from a mild stretch to a complete rupture, or avulsion (tearing of the tendinous tissue away from its place of insertion). The exact cause of the muscle strain is often very difficult to ascertain, but often it is a breakdown in the reciprocal coordination of one agonist muscle group and its antagonist or opposing muscle group, such as commonly caused by faulty postural alignment. Factors such as muscle fatigue or muscle imbalance caused by poor conditioning habits are frequently to blame for strains. Muscle cramping that results from profuse sweating and mineral loss can produce muscle tears.

Muscle strain intensity can be graded according to standards of mild, moderate, and severe or first, second, and third degree. In dancers the most common sites of strains are in the legs and lower trunk regions. However, strains also can occur in the low back, shoulder girdle, and neck. First-degree strains are usually associated with mild spasm and soreness that are usually not noticed until the day following the injury. In most cases of mild strain the causative factor is muscle spasm, not tearing or overstretching of the tissue. In second-degree strain the dancer usually senses the muscle tissue giving way or tearing, followed by spasm, pain, weakness, and loss of function in the area. There may be a sharp pain or burning sensation immediately following the occurrence of this strain. Feeling, or palpating, the part discloses point tenderness accompanied by a muscle contraction and swelling. When the tissue has been ruptured, an indentation may be felt. The severe or third-degree strain displays immediate severe pain, burning sensation, loss of function, and point tenderness. Whenever a third-degree strain is detected, especially if there is severe loss of function that lasts for a long period of time in the affected part, medical attention must be obtained immediately.

Although less common than the strain, a *sprain* is one of the most disabling injuries that can occur to the dancer. A sprain is a wrenching of a joint that produces a stretching or tearing of the joint's stabilizing connective tissue. When the joint is forced beyond its anatomical limits, the articular capsule, synovial membrane, and tendons can be affected. The sprain is associated with varying degrees of joint swelling, tenderness, and loss of function and, like the contusion and strain, can be categorized as first, second, or third degree. The first-degree sprain involves slight stretching of the connective tissue with very little loss of function and perhaps a twinge of pain when the joint is twisted. The moderate sprain is much more severe, often taking up to 2 or 3 weeks to heal. The third-degree sprain is a serious condition and normally involves a great deal of swelling and loss of joint function. A third-degree sprain may be almost a dislocation of the joint.

A *dislocation* is a disunion of one bone in its relationship to another bone, resulting in extensive pathologic damage. A dislocation must always be considered at least as serious as a fractured bone. The dislocated joint is best recognized by its deformity and should be automatically referred to a physician for medical treatment.

A *fracture* is a disruption of a bone's continuity. Although relatively uncommon in dance, there are situations in which fractures can be incurred. For example, the dancer can fall from a height, suddenly twist a part, or spontaneously fracture an area that has become overstressed or fatigued. In the most severe cases of fracture, jagged bone ends can protrude through the skin, causing both internal and external pathologic damage. All severe musculoskeletal dance injuries should be considered fractures and routinely referred to a physician for diagnosis. Fracture signs are deformity, rapid swelling, extreme tenderness at the site, and partial or complete loss of function. A fracture site in some cases may appear as an extra joint and produce a grating sound when moved. All suspected fractures should be splinted, including the joints above and below the injury site, to ensure proper stabilization.

Chronic musculoskeletal problems

As discussed earlier, the acute injury is one that comes on suddenly and, if cared for properly, is resolved quickly. On the other hand, an acute injury that is not properly managed in its early stages or that is aggravated by repeated injury may become chronic. A chronic problem is defined as one that has a gradual onset and long duration. The chronic problem, whether it originates from a contusion, strain, or sprain, represents a constant irritation with a low-grade inflammatory state usually associated with a great deal of scarring. At all costs the dancer should avoid repeated injuries to any area in an attempt to prevent a chronic condition. The chronic problem is often named for the tissue that it is associated with, such as bursitis, myositis, fasciitis, periostitis, or tendinitis.

Once a chronic problem has been incurred, it must be cared for by conservative means. This usually includes rest and elimination of further aggravation combined with appropriate physical therapy and supportive procedures. The dancer should be apprised that once a chronic problem has been incurred, there is usually a tendency for recurrence under similar conditions.

Shock

The problem of shock must be included in a discussion of injuries to the musculoskeletal system. Shock must always be interpreted as a sign of severe injury. It is related to the injury proper and also to the psychological manifestations that often accompany a traumatic situation. Shock occurs as the result of a diminished amount of fluid in the circulatory system that inhibits the red blood cells from adequately distributing oxygen throughout the body. When shock occurs, plasma (the fluid part of the circulatory system) is lost into the outside tissue spaces, leaving the solid particles within the blood vessels unable to flow adequately throughout the body. When shock occurs, there is usually a drop in blood pressure and the pulse becomes weak, shallow, and rapid, often causing the dancer to become lightheaded and nauseous. Any moderate to severe injury can bring about physiological shock; however, fear and emotional upset about an injury can also cause shock to happen.

Those helping the injured dancer should always expect shock when a serious injury is present and act accordingly. Under these circumstances the dancer should be maintained in a reclining position with the head and trunk level, the lower limbs elevated slightly, and the body temperature kept as normal as possible. For the highly sensitive individual who has a fear of injury or an extremely low pain threshold, it is desirable to keep spectators away and to keep an unsightly injury covered. Medical attention should be obtained as soon as possible.

chapter eight

Therapeutics

The dancer or the teacher of dance should be able to provide proper first aid in cases of injury and be able to initiate an effective therapeutic program for injuries of a less serious nature. Many therapeutic approaches can be extremely beneficial in assisting nature. The primary therapeutic approaches that will be discussed are cold, heat, analgesic balm and liniment, massage, exercise, supportive and protective techniques, and medical care.

Cold

Cold (cryotherapy) has been mentioned in previous chapters as being extremely important in the immediate care of a musculoskeletal injury. However, cold can also be used as a follow-up therapy technique. Cold is becoming very popular as a therapeutic agent and is very often used in preference to heat. It is difficult to determine from research exactly what happens physiologically when cold is applied to the skin; however, it is generally agreed that cold initially constricts blood vessels and reduces spasm in a particular area. If cold is applied for 20 minutes or longer, vasoconstriction changes to vasodilation, followed by an increase of circulation in the deeper tissues.

The dancer will find cold application important in constricting superficial blood vessels and inhibiting local blood circulation immediately following an injury. Cold combined with compression and elevation of the part tends to localize internal hemorrhaging and helps in resolution of the injury. In terms of follow-up therapeutic care, ice is extremely valuable when a spasm is present. Cold application reduces spasm and the associated pain by reducing pressure on the pain receptors.

Cold can be applied in many forms by the dancer himself (Fig. 8-1). Cold packs can be made by placing ice in a towel, or for the dancer who will be in a place where a cold medium is not available, a chemical cold pack can be purchased. When mixed with water the pack readily becomes cold and lasts about 30 minutes. Ice water immersion with water temperatures approximately 60° or 65° F. is a good means of producing analgesia or inhibiting pain in the area.

A technique that has become popular in the care of muscle injuries is ice

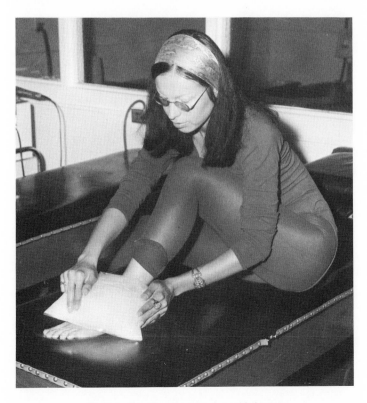

Fig. 8-1. Use of an ice pack for cold therapy.

massage (Fig. 8-2). Ice massage is utilized by freezing water in a paper cup and then tearing off the paper, producing a cylinder of ice. One thickness of a towel is wrapped around the ice, which is used to make small circular movements over the affected part until three important steps are experienced. Step one is the sensation of cold, step two is the sensation of mild aching, in which the skin turns a bright red, and step three is the numbing stage. When the part has reached the numb stage it is put into a gradual stretch, which is maintained for 1 or 2 minutes and repeated several times a day. The ice massage technique reduces spasm and assists in increasing the mobility of the part. Because it is readily accessible and inexpensive, ice massage is one of the most valuable of cold therapy techniques.

Heat

Heat has been used for therapy since recorded time. It provides a pain-reducing effect, speeds up circulation, encourages venous and lymphatic drainage, and speeds up metabolism, thus encouraging the healing process. Because of its soothing effect when first applied, the dancer may prefer heat over cold therapy.

Superficial heating occurs on the surface of the skin, in contrast to deep

Fig. 8-2. Application of ice massage to a swollen knee.

heating, which acts deep within the body's tissues. Both forms will be discussed, but the dancer must realize that deep heating is in the province of physical therapy and must be conducted under supervision of a physician. On the other hand, superficial heating can be safely initiated by the dancer if reasonable procedures are followed.

Superficial heat therapy

Superficial heat therapy can come in many forms. Probably the most common forms are the heat that is generated from an electric pad and the heat that comes from a bathtub or shower. A very popular device is the moist heat pad shown in Fig. 8-3. Unlike cold therapy, heat should never be applied to an injured part when there is hemorrhaging in the area. Sometimes as long as 3 days should elaspe following an injury before heat is applied.

Heat therapy should start at lower temperatures and be gradually increased daily. Immersion baths, in which the injured part is placed in warm water, can eventually go as high as 120° F. with immersion for 10 to 30 minutes, depending on the individual's skin sensitivity. However, it is suggested that an immersion bath start with temperatures around 90° F. An important type of immersion bath is the whirlpool, or hydromassage, which may or may not be accessible to

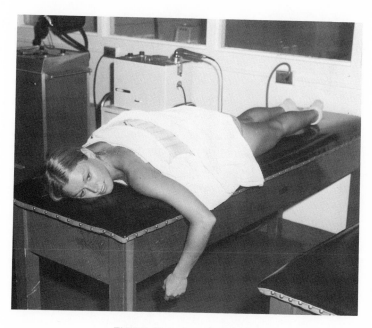

Fig. 8-3. Moist heat therapy.

the dancer (Fig. 8-4). The whirlpool is one of the most popular forms of hydrotherapy. The whirlpool combines the heat and soothing effect of the water with an agitation or massage action that mildly increases circulation. Like the immersion bath, the whirlpool should start out at lower temperatures; a good beginning is an initial exposure of no longer than 10 minutes at a temperature of 90°. The whirlpool temperature should never be above 100° to 105° F. and should last no longer than 10 to 20 minutes. If the body is fully submerged to the neck in the whirlpool tub, exposure should not exceed 10 minutes at 100° F.

The contrasting technique, which alternates hot and cold water soaks, has been used for many years to relieve swelling and muscle spasm. This technique is excellent for injuries that are 3 or 4 days old and centered around major joints such as the ankle and knee. The dancer prepares two tubs of water, one with a temperature of 105° F. and the other with a temperature of 60° F. The procedure starts with alternately soaking the part in the hot water for 5 minutes

Fig. 8-4. Hydromassage in a whirlpool bath.

and in the cold tub for 2 minutes and then continuing to alternately soak the part 4 minutes in the hot water and 2 minutes in the cold. The entire contrast therapy regime continues for approximately 30 minutes, with the last cycle finishing in the hot tub.

There are many other superficial therapeutic heat techniques that would be beneficial. However, those that have been discussed are the most readily used by highly active people. Ideally, heat therapy should be initiated two or three times daily. However, precautions must be taken against overexposing the injury to temperature extremes for long periods of time. For example, sensitive body tissue should always be protected by a cloth material before a hot pad or cold therapy is applied to the skin. In the case of the hydromassage, the jet stream should never be directed to the injured part, but should be aimed at the side of the tub, with the circulation occurring secondarily around the injured member.

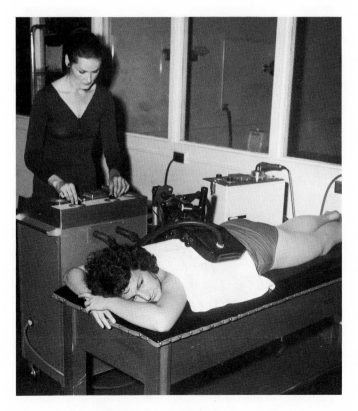

Fig. 8-5. Short-wave diathermy.

Deep heat therapy

It is readily apparent that a book of this type is not intended to give the reader definitive information on physical therapy techniques. This is particularly true when discussing the deep heat therapies. It is important, though, that a dancer have some understanding of the deep therapies to appreciate the medical implications of their use.

The two most common deep heat modalities are diathermy and ultrasound. Diathermy is the use of high-frequency electric current as a therapeutic aid (Fig. 8-5). In general the waves penetrate the skin and generate heat from the bone outward, raising the internal temperature as much as 9° F. On the other hand, ultrasound therapy consists of an electric generator that produces a micro-massage action on the patient through a sound head containing a quartz crystal (Fig. 8-6). Ultrasound must be applied to the injured area through a liquid

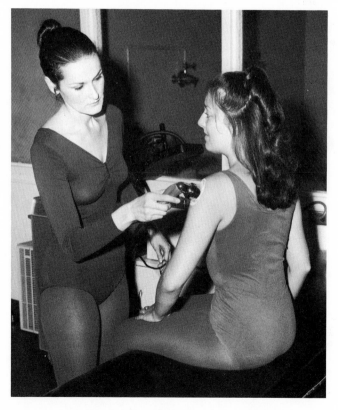

Fig. 8-6. Ultrasound therapy.

medium such as mineral oil or water and can raise the internal temperature of the part from 7° to 8° F. Although each physician and physical therapist has his own preference as to the use of these modalities, diathermy is often used in areas of high fluid content such as a muscle belly. On the other hand, ultrasound therapy is very often used in areas where there is great density of tissue such as fascia and ligaments.

When discussing deep therapy, one must also include muscle stimulation, as it is widely used in the rehabilitation of injured muscles. Depending on the current used in physical therapy, varying physiological responses can be produced. An alternating (faradic) current produces an intermittent flow of electric current to the muscles and assists in preventing atrophy. The other commonly used current is sinusoidal, a gradual and rhythmical current with rising and falling intensity. It can produce mild exercise of a part as well as assist in relaxation of tense and fatigued muscles. Muscle stimulation applied to the healthy individual with normal muscles that have become injured cannot be compared to active exercise for rehabilitation.

Analgesic balm and liniment

Although not actually heat media, analgesic balm and liniment are often used to bring about much the same effect as superficial heat therapy. Used extensively in athletics, the analgesic balm pack provides therapy while the individual is moving. The technique is to apply a petroleum-based rubefacient to the injury after the acute stage has passed. A rubefacient is a substance that provides a mild irritation to the skin, bringing about a mild increase in circulation and analgesia. The rubefacients that are commonly found in analgesic balms are oil of wintergreen, red pepper, and menthol. The balm is applied either directly to the skin or to some material, preferably cotton cloth, over which is placed a plastic sandwich wrapper or paper held in place by an elastic wrap around the entire part. This mild skin irritant counters the sense of pain, allowing the dancer with a mild injury to perform without undue discomfort. This practice, of course, should be discouraged in cases of serious injury where pain may be masked by the analgesic balm pack, placing the dancer in a situation in which additional injury might occur.

Massage

Massage is one of man's oldest therapeutic modalities. Most cultures, both ancient and modern, have employed this means as a health aid. The therapeutic massage used today in the United States has its origins in the work of Mitzger of Holland and Ling of Sweden. Massage is usually done passively on the patient by another person; however, a person can also apply massage to himself in some areas of the body. Massage is an inexpensive and readily available therapy technique. Physiologically, massage can encourage venous and lymphatic drainage, stretch soft tissue, increase nutrition and metabolism to a given area, and assist in removing waste products more readily. Depending on the technique employed, massage can relax or stimulate the body.

Many factors must be taken into consideration for effective massage. Most techniques of massage use a friction-proofing medium to prevent skin and hair from pulling, such as cold cream, mineral oil, or talcum powder. Effective massage must have the body placed in a completely relaxed position. If the body is tense, the effect of the massage may be completely nullified.

The three most prevalent techniques used in massage therapy are effleurage, pétrissage, and friction techniques. Effleurage is either light or deep stroking (Fig. 8-7). Light stroking is designed to relax or bring about a sedative response. Deep stroking is designed to compress and to increase the venous and lymphatic circulation of the massaged part. Both types of effleurage may be used

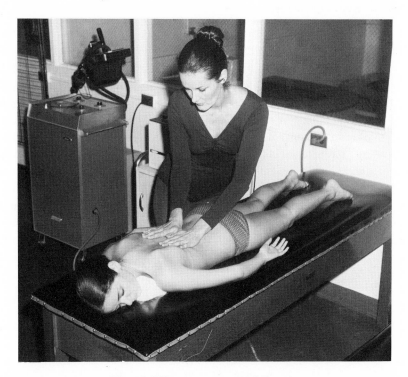

Fig. 8-7. Effleurage massage technique.

alternately on the dancer. Effleurage is applied differently to different parts of the body. For example, when stroking the back, the operator starts in the low back region and moves upward along the spine to the tops of the shoulder, applying constant pressure with the heels of the hands. When the hands have reached the top of the shoulders, they move outward from the spine about ½ inch on each side and then trail down, with the fingertips returning to the starting point. This procedure is continued until the hands have traveled the full width and length of the back, then the hands are moved from the outside of the back inward, tracing the area of the back that has already been covered. In massaging the back the operator may also want to add a lift and roll when the trapezius muscle has been reached. This is known as trapezial milking. The effleurage stroke should be slow and rhythmical in every respect and should last no longer than 5 to 7 minutes on any given part of the body.

In the effleurage technique for the shoulder and arm the dancer lies with the affected side facing the operator. In this position the affected shoulder or arm is relaxed and readily available for massage. The massage starts high up on the

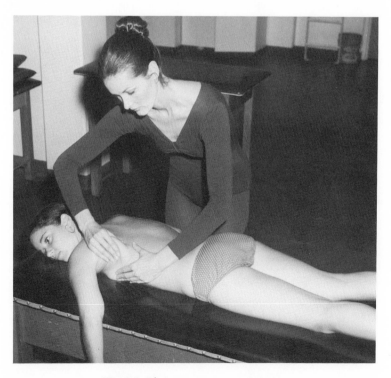

Fig. 8-8. Pétrissage massage technique.

shoulder area, with the arm resting over the operator's shoulder. The operator's hands travel up over the top of the deltoid muscle, over the back of the scapula, and in front of the pectoralis area. The hands stroke upward and then trail downward, overlapping the preceding stroke about ½ to 1 inch and then stroking upward over the same area. In this manner, each tissue area is massaged again and again. A complete massage stroke moves from the fingertips up and over the wrist, forearm, and upper arm, and then over the shoulder complex.

Effleurage to the lower limb follows the same principles. The leg and thigh are put in a comfortable position, with the lower leg slightly elevated and the feet resting on a pillow. It is started just below the buttocks, with the stroke moving over the buttocks and the lower back region. As in the massage of the arm, each subsequent stroke is started below the previous stroke until the entire leg has been rubbed. In this manner, congestants are carried by the circulatory system back to the heart for cleansing.

Pétrissage is therapeutic kneading designed to loosen and decongest a particular tissue region (Fig. 8-8). It is best executed in bulky tissue areas such as the trapezius, buttocks, thighs, and triceps. The massage technique is one of lifting, pulling, rolling, and twisting the tissue without pinching it. Pétrissage is a

Fig. 8-9. Friction massage technique.

fairly vigorous technique that should only be employed when injuries have been fully resolved.

Friction is an excellent technique for massaging body tissue close to bone, such as around joints, and for relieving muscle spasms (Fig. 8-9). This technique is designed to increase local circulation while at the same time stretching underlying tissue. The technique is executed by bracing the heels of the hand while the fingers make circles in opposite directions. The fingers can also be braced to free the thumbs for massaging.

Effleurage, pétrissage, and friction techniques are particularly applicable to the problems that face dancers. They can be employed easily by other dancers or in some cases by the dancer himself. (Purposefully not discussed here are the techniques of percussion or tapotment. Percussion massage, which commonly includes the techniques of slapping, hacking, and cupping, is not considered therapeutic.) The dancer should be warned that massage is contraindicated when an injury is still hemorrhaging. If there is doubt about the resolution of an injury, massage should be applied above and below the injury site. When it is certain that the injury is not hemorrhaging, then massage should begin over the injured site, lightly at first and then progressively harder. Also, massage should never be used as a means to warm up in place of the regular warm-up procedures. However, it is valuable as a means of stretching and loosening an injured area in conjunction with the warm-up regime. A general body massage will assist the dancer who feels fatigue or stiffness due to congested muscles.

Exercise

Exercise properly executed is one of the most important therapeutic modalities. There are two exercise considerations that are important to the dancer who is attempting to recover from a musculoskeletal injury. These considerations are divided into a generalized exercise program and a specific therapeutic exercise program.

A *general program of exercise* should be instituted in order to prevent deconditioning that comes from inactivity. The reconditioning program following an injury includes exercising the entire body with the exception of the specific injured part, which is isolated from activity until it can engage in a specific therapeutic regime. A dancer who suffers from a severe infection, is debilitated because of fatigue, or has some chronic inflammatory condition must avoid the general conditioning program. It is commonly known that prolonged inactivity results in a general lack of physical strength and muscle atrophy. If confined to a bed for a long time, the dancer will also experience a demineralization of bones. The reconditioning program should develop all the physical fitness attributes of strength, flexibility, endurance, and the maintenance of coordination without aggravating the injured part.

Following the initiating of a generalized exercise program, if the injured dancer is to return to full function as soon as possible, a therapeutic exercise of the injured part should be initiated. However, the specific therapeutic exercises must not adversely affect the injury. Therapeutic exercises are applied as soon as the obvious acute stages, particularly pain, have diminished.

Therapeutic exercise, like the general exercise program, involves four primary factors: strength, flexibility, muscle endurance, and coordination. Each of these qualities must be restored to the part before the dancer may safely return to a full activity program. Reconditioning exercises will be discussed more fully in Part 5.

Supportive and protective techniques

It is important that a dancer have a working knowledge of the values and uses of various materials that can protect and support the body in an injury situation. The areas discussed in this book are thought to be the most important and practical to dance. These include the various types of bandages, adhesive tape, and padding techniques.

Bandages

The dancer should have some knowledge of the variety and purpose of the available bandages. The most common type of bandages used are the triangular, the cravat, and the roller bandage. The triangular and cravat bandages are used mainly in first-aid situations and most commonly in cases of arm or shoulder injuries. A cervical sling is make by positioning the triangular bandage under the injured arm with its apex facing the elbow (Fig. 8-10). The end of the triangle closest to the body is carried over the shoulder of the injured arm while the other end is allowed to hang down loosely. Then the loose end is pulled over the shoulder on the uninjured side and the two ends of the bandage are tied in a square knot behind the neck. The end of the bandage that sticks out at the elbow is then brought around to the side of the elbow and pinned.

The roller bandage, which can be made from different materials and in a variety of widths, is probably the most handy of the available types of bandages. It comes in gauze, cotton cloth, and elastic material as well as in many synthetic materials applicable to almost any part of the body.

Some general rules that apply to any type of roller bandage are as follows:
1. Hold the roller bandage in the preferred hand with the loose end extending from the bottom of the cylinder.

Fig. 8-10. Cervical sling.

2. Constant pressure should be applied on the bandage throughout the entire procedure.

3. The wrap must be tight enough to be held firmly in place, but not so tight that it impedes circulation.

4. Each turn of the wrap should overlap at least half the width of the preceding turn, ensuring that the wrap will not separate and expose the skin.

5. Ideally, if the wrap is to cover a large area, it is best to start the wrap at the smallest circumference and wrap toward the largest circumference of the part.

6. The wrap should be secured by being tied or held firmly with adhesive tape; however, the end of the wrap should never be at the site of the injury.

FIGURE-OF-EIGHT, SPICA, AND SPIRAL BANDAGES. The figure-of-eight and spica bandages are the most practical for active persons. When elastic wrap material is used the figure-of-eight and spica serve to hold dressings in place, to provide mild soft tissue support, and to allow for full movement by the individual without fear of the bandage becoming loose. The elastic bandage is sometimes used over strapping to provide additional support. Both the figure-of-eight and spica are executed in the same manner, except that the spica has a larger loop on one end. Although spica or figure-of-eight bandages can be placed on any joint of the body, they are mainly used on the ankle, foot, hip, knee, shoulder, and elbow.

Ankle and foot spica (Fig. 8-11). A 2-inch elastic bandage is anchored around the metatarsal arch; then it is brought across the instep, around and behind the heel, and back across the instep to return to the metatarsal. The procedure is repeated with the wrap moved continuously upward until the entire foot has been covered. Extra material is wrapped around the ankle.

Spiral bandage (Fig. 8-12). The spiral bandage is utilized often in dance to assist with problems of the leg, thigh, and occasionally the lower and upper arms. The material of choice for the spiral is the elastic wrap, between 2 and 3 inches in width depending on the size of the dancer and the area to be covered. The spiral bandage is anchored at the smallest circumference of the part and usually proceeds upward against gravity in a spiral fashion. When using the

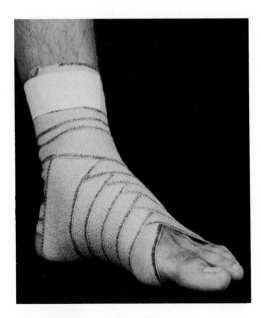

Fig. 8-11. Ankle and foot spica.

elastic wrap, it is best to anchor the spiral by starting the technique at one angle and then, as the wrap is brought around the part, changing the direction of the angle. In this manner the wrap will be firmly anchored and not slip as it proceeds in a spiral manner upward in consecutive turns. Spiraling should continue upward above the injured site and then proceed downward. A good rule of thumb in completing the spiral wrap is to never go down as far as the starting point and never go up as far as the end point, but concentrate the spirals in the center of the wrapped limb.

Knee figure-of-eight bandage. The knee is a difficult joint to wrap effectively. A spiral bandage is often preferred over the figure-of-eight because it is easier to apply and seems to stay in place better during activity. However, the figure-of-eight should be used when complete freedom of movement is desired. The knee figure-of-eight bandage is best used to secure a dressing on either the front or the back of the knee or when compression is desired over a swollen area. The bandage is anchored by encircling the lower leg. The wrap is then brought upward across either the kneecap or the back of the knee and around the thigh. It is subsequently carried downward, crossing the kneecap again. This procedure is continued until all the material has been applied.

Hip spica (Fig. 8-13). The hip spica is one of the most practical wraps used in

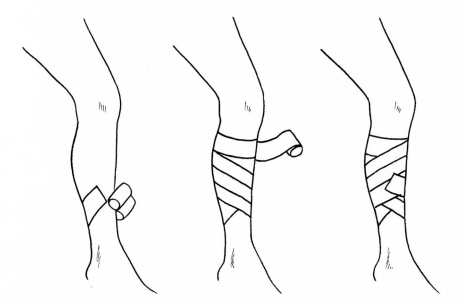

Fig. 8-12. Spiral elastic wrap technique.

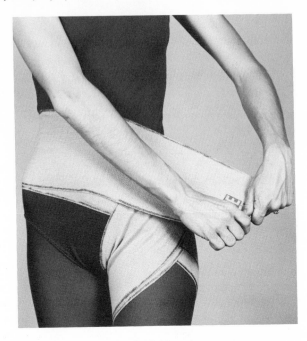

Fig. 8-13. Hip spica.

dance. It serves to provide mild pressure and support to the hip and groin muscles as well as to efficiently hold a heat or ice pad over the injury site. Because of the limited amount of material, the hip spica technique must be well planned and executed. The end of a 6-inch elastic wrap is placed at a point on the upper thigh over the injured site. Anchoring is initiated by encircling the thigh, then moving up the thigh to the groin, across the lower abdominal area, and around the crest of the ilium. The wrap is then continued around the low back and crossed over the thigh.

Shoulder spica (Fig. 8-14). Although used less commonly than the other figure-of-eight and spica wraps mentioned, the shoulder spica is a technique that dancers will find a need for if a strain of the shoulder occurs and a mild support is needed. Before the shoulder is wrapped, the underarm should be well padded to prevent constriction of blood vessels. The wrap is started at the midpoint of the deltoid region and proceeds around in back of the underarm, in front of the deltoid, around the back underneath the unaffected arm, and around the chest to the starting point. In wrapping the shoulder it is imperative that the dancer maintain good posture with shoulders held in proper alignment.

Elbow figure-of-eight bandage (Fig. 8-15). Like the shoulder spica, the elbow

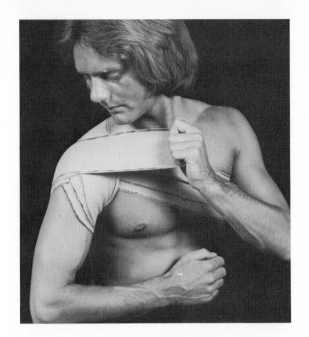

Fig. 8-14. Shoulder spica.

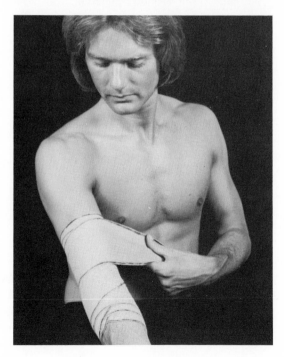

Fig. 8-15. Elbow figure-of-eight.

figure-of-eight will only occasionally be needed. It is similar in pattern to the knee figure-of-eight, the bandage being anchored by encircling the lower arm with one complete turn. It then crosses either in front of or in back of the elbow and is carried upward to encircle the upper arm one complete turn. The pattern is continued with the wrap always moving toward the center of the joint, ending at the upper arm area.

Adhesive tape

Adhesive tape is being used increasingly in the prevention and protection of injuries to active persons. There are a great many types of adhesive tapes now available to the consumer. The two most popular types are the rigid nonyielding linen-backed tape and the elastic tape. Both have a special importance in the prevention and care of injuries. In recent years the production of special light-weight athletic tape has become a boon to active people. Many of these tapes on the market are both lightweight and strong. Three features make up the best quality of athletic tape: backing, mass, and unwinding properties. When properly applied, the lightweight tape can provide a high degree of strength and protection for the dancer and is much preferred over heavier tape. For the person who is going to wear tape for a long period of time, it is important that the adhesive mass be of high quality with the ability to resist profuse perspiration, body heat, and movement. The tape mass must not irritate the skin nor leave a residue on the skin when removed. It is also important that tape unwind evenly throughout the entire roll. It is difficult, if not impossible, to properly apply tape that has variable unwinding qualities.

Before tape is applied the skin surface must be properly prepared. Perspiration and dirt as well as hair must be removed. For good tape adherence and the elimination of irritation, the skin surface should be sprayed with a commercial tape adherent that provides a tacky residue and has toughening qualities. For skin that is extremely sensitive to tape or for skin areas that must remain taped for a long period of time, there is now available an underwrap material that provides a thin yet snugly fitting covering on the skin to be taped (Fig. 8-16).

When tape is applied to the body, many factors must be taken into consideration in order to ensure proper support and the elimination of irritation. The more angular the part to be taped, the narrower should be the tape and vice versa. For example, ½-inch to 1-inch tape should be used for hands and feet, while 1½-inch tape is best for knees, and 2-inch tape can be used for the low back and other expansive body regions. In cases where a body part is to be supported by strapping, it must be placed in the most neutral position possible.

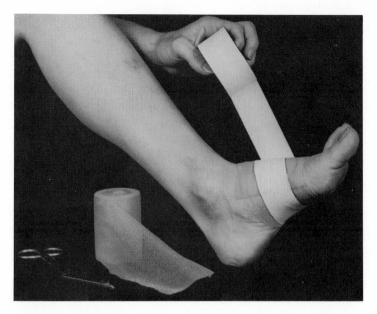

Fig. 8-16. Protective underwrap material for skin protection during strapping.

When tape is overlapped, it is best to overlap at least one half the width of the preceding tape layer. The dancer should note that tape must never be continuously wrapped around a part, but should be torn each time a circle is executed. Tearing after each circle avoids losing control of the tape and prevents application that might be too tight. Tape should be molded and smoothed as it is applied, one piece at a time. It is desirable to allow the tape to conform to the natural contours of the body. Tape adheres to tape better than to skin; consequently, most techniques employed in taping should have an anchor strip at the beginning and a lock strip after applying a particular pattern. Although there are many types of underwraps (such as gauzes, pads, stockinettes, and prewrap materials), the dancer should realize that the best support is afforded by tape applied directly over skin.

Padding

There are many protective and supportive devices available to the dancer other than bandages and adhesive tapes. These devices can be purchased commercially or they can be constructed out of a variety of materials. In dance, padding is primarily utilized for foot problems and is designed to brace, protect, or reestablish normal weight bearing. The most common materials utilized are moleskin (felt with an adhesive mass backing), sponge with an adhesive backing, and chiropodist felt (⅛-inch felt material that also has an adhesive backing). In most cases pads should be custom made because commercial pads are not usually sufficiently durable to withstand the great forces that are produced by the dancer. Caution should be taken that the wearing of commercial orthopedic pads or braces does not force the dancer's body out of normal postural balance. If this does occur, other tissue breakdown may be expected in other parts of the body. More details will be given on specific protective and supportive devices in Part 5.

Medical care

It is often difficult for the dancer to know when a physician should be contacted following injury. Fear of pain or fear of being kept out of dance activity often causes the dancer to wait too long before seeking professional help. Therefore it is desirable for the dancer to seek help from a doctor who empathizes with the very active individual. Obviously the active, healthy person reacts much differently to an injury than one who is sedentary or elderly. The less active individual might profit by many days or even weeks of conservative care, while the dancer may become psychologically depressed by long periods of inactivity. Because the dancer responds much more quickly to treatment than does the sedentary individual, it is obvious that a physician who understands and is sympathetic to the highly active person should be sought.

In cases of musculoskeletal injury the physician usually wants to have an x-ray film taken in order to discount the possibility of fracture. X-ray examinations are routine for injuries of the joints because of the high probability of fracture in those areas. Even though an x-ray film cannot indicate or detect ligamentous tears, it can show the physician the amount of abnormal laxity present in a particular joint when the joint is stressed. In dance, fractures usually occur spontaneously, particularly under fatigue conditions. Muscles can also pull away pieces of bone if a contraction is strong enough. In both instances, x-ray examination could determine the extent of injury.

All physicians have their own ways of caring for injuries. Many vary in their use of medications, depending on the successes they have had in the past and on their educational backgrounds. For example, a serious musculoskeletal injury may call for a general anesthetic such as meperidine (Demerol) to relieve pain and spasm. This is often the initial drug of choice because of its particular reaction on the nervous system in relieving pain and muscle spasticity. A musculoskeletal injury may require a specific muscle relaxant that assists the injury by reducing muscle spasm and therefore relieving pressure on pain receptors.

In acute situations the physician normally prefers to give a muscle relaxant within the first 24 hours after injury; however, relaxants may also be given in cases where a chronic condition is present.

Enzyme drugs are also currently used by many physicians as therapeutic agents in the initial phase of an acute injury. Enzyme drugs are catalytic agents that change chemical reactions without being affected in the process. Introducing enzyme drugs to the newly injured individual has many advantages: sometimes the physician desires to decrease the viscosity of the fluid in the injured area or, on the other hand, to increase the rate of digestion of proteins, particularly blood clots and other waste materials. Other enzymes may assist in overcoming the inflammatory process following trauma. Not all physicians believe that enzyme drugs work effectively on all people, although many believe that it is worth trying enzymes.

The chronic musculoskeletal condition presents a different set of problems to the physician. Often, rest and anti-inflammatory agents are the only alternatives left to the physician because the person with a chronic problem has a constant low-grade inflammation. The anti-inflammatory agent is introduced to the dancer to help the body in overcoming this problem. Cortisone or cortisonelike substances often are prescribed. Cortisone is a hormone that is normally produced by the cortex of the adrenal gland. It is widely taken by injection or orally to assist this normal bodily reaction in combating difficult chronic conditions. This procedure has been particularly beneficial in such problems as arthritis, degenerative joint diseases and other musculoskeletal diseases. Often cortisone is used in conjunction with such physical therapy modalities as ultrasound therapy; when combined, they raise the metabolism of a given area and decrease the accumulation of fibrous scar tissue.

part five

Common dance conditions

Part 5 is concerned with the most prevalent conditions that occur to dancers. The following chapters give up-to-date information on the prevention and care of injuries resulting from compression, friction, strain, sprain, dislocation, and fractures.

chapter nine

Compression
and friction injuries

Traumatic compression of tissue or friction is a common occurrence for the active person. Either striking with the body itself or being hit by some outside source can cause tissue to be contused. Compression of the tissue can be a single event causing acute inflammatory conditions with hemorrhage, pain, swelling, and malfunction. Or the result of repeated traumatic events can be a chronic irritation such as that produced by abnormal pressures of poorly fitting shoes or the chronic compressions that come from faulty body alignment.

Contusions (Table 1)

Contusions or bruises that arise from a blow to the body can occur to any part of the dancer's anatomy. However, they most often happen to the leg or foot region. The body's reaction to contusion is dependent on the body site and its particular sensitivity. Extremely sensitive body areas are located on the inner thigh, the face, the skin, the heel, and bony protruberences. The more resilient soft tissue such as found in the thigh region and calf can withstand a greater blow than, for example, the skin or heel of the foot.

Table 1. Acute contusion management*

Degree of injury	Basic signs	Treatment program				
		Management phase	Physical therapy	Dosage	Reconditioning	Dosage
First degree	Mild blow to the body from an outside source causing abnormal tissue compression with little pathologic damage; some muscle spasm may be present	Step 1: immediate care	1. Cold, pressure if pain symptoms last more than a few minutes	½-1 hr.	1. Gradual stretch following cold and pressure	Symptomatic
Second degree	Moderate blow to the body resulting in a bruise with pain, loss of function, point tenderness, and muscle spasm lasting from several minutes to several hours; swelling and discoloration may occur if proper immediate treatment is not given	Step 1: immediate care	1. Cold, pressure; 20 min. on, 10 min. off 2. Elevation 3. May warrant referral to physician for medication	2-24 hr. 2-hr.	1. Gradual stretch following application of cold	2-3 min. twice daily
		Step 2: second day	1. Start program of gradual heating with warm water soak (100° F.) or whirlpool (90° F.) 2. Wear elastic wrap for support	15 min. twice daily	1. Avoid activity of part until hemorrhage has ceased 2. Continue gradual stretch after physical therapy 3. General exercise without aggravation of injury	Twice daily

	Step 3: third or fourth day	1. Superficial and deep heat may be applied, e.g., water soak (120° F.) or whirlpool (105° F.)	20 min. three times daily	1. Gradually begin to exercise injury while wearing elastic wrap; do not exercise if pain is present	Three times daily
		2. Diathermy	As prescribed	2. Dancer is well when part is pain free	
		3. Wear elastic wrap	Three times daily		
		4. If spasm is present use ice massage	When active		
		5. Analgesic balm pack			
Third degree	*Severe* blow to the body resulting in extreme pain, loss of function, point tenderness, and muscle spasm lasting for several hours or longer; swelling and discoloration are common even with proper immediate care	Step 1: immediate care	1. Cold, pressure; 20 min. on, 10 min. off	24-48 hr.	1. Gradual stretch *only* after a 24 hr. period has passed	2-3 min. twice daily
		2. Elevation of part			
		3. Refer to physician for examination and medication	24 hr.		
		4. Wear elastic wrap			
		Step 2: third or fourth day	1. Start gradual heat program with warm water soak (100° F.) or whirlpool (90° F.)	15 min. twice daily	1. Do not exercise injured part	Twice daily
		2. Continue to wear elastic wrap		2. General exercise	
				3. Gradual stretch after therapy	
		Step 3: fourth or fifth day	1. See step 3 of second-degree contusion		1. Dancer has recovered when part is pain free and has regained full strength and flexibility	

*Adapted from Klafs, C. E., and Arnheim, D. D.: Modern Principles of athletic training, ed. 3, St. Louis, 1973, The C. V. Mosby Co.

Generally speaking, contusions can be classified as first, second, and third degree. The first-degree or mild contusion has symptoms of minimal pain and some point tenderness lasting for a very short time. Consequently, the first-degree contusion normally produces little inflammation, with most of the discomfort, if any, coming from muscle spasm. To avoid swelling and discoloration, the dancer should apply cold and pressure followed by a gradual stretch to relieve muscle spasm. If discomfort lasts more than a few minutes, it may be advisable to apply an elastic wrap for the remainder of the day. It is doubtful that a first-degree contusion would prevent the dancer from continuing activity the next day. If some swelling and irritation are apparent the next day, it is advisable to start a program of warm water soaks or whirlpool baths with temperatures not exceeding 90° F.

The second-degree or moderate contusion results from a hard blow to the muscle tissue or bone, resulting in an immediate loss of function with a great deal of pain and tenderness on palpation. This degree of contusion, if occurring to very soft tissue, may cause an immediate swelling and perhaps discoloration the next day. Much of the discomfort comes from muscle spasm in the area. Immediate treatment should consist of cold and pressure by an elastic wrap applied intermittently for at least 24 hours. Elevation of the part may also be advisable if rapid swelling and discomfort are present. When muscle spasm is evident, the affected muscle should be placed in a static stretch position and the position maintained for at least 1 hour. If there is extreme loss of function, it may be advisable to refer the injury to a physician for possible medication, including a muscle relaxant and enzymes to more quickly assist injury resolution. If hemorrhage appears to be under control by the following day, a gradual program of heat therapy may be initiated. It is advisable that water soak therapy with temperatures not to exceed 90°F. be applied until the injury has ceased hemorrhaging. Following cold therapy, a very mild gradual stretch program will help alleviate muscle spasm and pain in the area. In cases where the moderate contusion causes the dancer to miss class for a number of days, it is advisable that a general exercise program be instituted to prevent deconditioning. However, exercising the contused area should be avoided until it is symptom free. If the dancer needs to move the injured part, an elastic wrap should be worn to prevent clot disruption and rehemorrhaging in the area. Therapeutic heat temperature should be gradually raised daily until whirlpool baths have reached 105° F. If water soaks are the treatment chosen, the temperature can be gradually raised to 120° F.

A third-degree contusion results from a severe and penetrating blow to the body. The result of this violent blow is extensive compression of soft tissue, producing muscle spasm and severe loss of function with extensive hemorrhaging and swelling. Because of the seriousness of this injury, a physician should be contacted to discount the possibility of fracture or muscle rupture. As in the moderate contusion, medication may be the choice of the physician for combating spasm and encouraging the speedy absorption of fluids associated with the injury. Immediate care includes cold, pressure, and elevation for up to 3 days or until hemorrhaging has fully ceased. Care is then similar to care of the moderate contusion: gradual heating is instituted and a graduated program of exercise is also begun.

Heel bruise

The calcaneal periostitis, or heel bruise, is one of the most handicapping acute injuries occurring to the active person. It is normally caused by stepping on a small object, overly compressing the tissue covering the heel bone (calcaneus), or by an abnormal shearing action of the skin covering the calcaneus. Some individuals are susceptible to the heel bruise because of having an irregularly shaped calcaneus. Because the dancer is unable to withstand the stresses of severe compression, whatever the cause, the heel bruise presents extreme pain and discomfort and in many cases completely prevents the dancer from placing the heel on the floor. Ideally, if a heel bruise is sustained, a cold compress should be applied immediately. However, it is discouraging to note that the heel bruise does not respond readily to most physical therapy procedures. If not reaggravated, this injury is self-limiting and will normally resolve itself in time. Because the dancer is usually unable to avoid weight bearing, in the case of heel bruise he should apply a protective strapping or padding to the heel region in an attempt to take the painful pressure off the bruise.

Various techniques can assist the dancer who is prone to heel bruises or currently experiencing one, such as the application of a doughnut cut from sponge rubber to assist in the equalization of pressures around the bruise and the application of a supportive strapping. The heel bruise strapping technique uses either 1- or ½-inch linen tape that is patterned into a basketweave cap around the heel (Fig. 9-1). The first piece of tape is placed at the base of the Achilles tendon, extending past both the internal and external ankle bones. The next tape piece is applied to the bottom of the heel, encircling it on both sides and finishing at the ends of the first strip. Tape is applied alternately until a complete cap has been applied to the heel.

A second site where bone bruises are prevalent is at the center of the metatarsal arch. Dancers who place a great deal of pressure on the ball of the

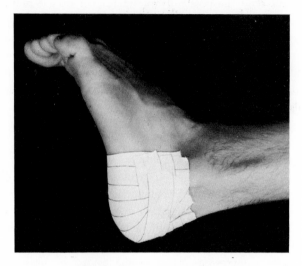

Fig. 9-1. Heel cap with 1-inch tape.

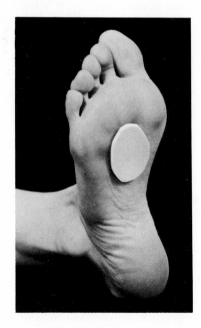

Fig. 9-2. Metatarsal arch pad.

foot often cause a bruise in this area. This problem is accentuated by a fallen metatarsal arch because weight bearing, instead of being on two points of the ball joint, is abnormally applied to three sites. The fallen metatarsal arch is prone to bruising when there is abnormal pressure as occurs in stepping on a small hard object. The metatarsal bruise can be relieved by a pad placed at the base of the metatarsal arch (Fig. 9-2). The metatarsal pad reestablishes the arch, relieving pressure on the bruise area. A pad can be made from many different materials but is most successful with either adhesive felt, ¼-inch thick, or adhesive sponge rubber. The dancer should cut an oval approximately 1½ inches in diameter and position the pad at the base of the metatarsal arch with a piece of 1-inch tape encircling the foot and holding the pad in place.

Chronic compression problems (Table 2)

Abnormal pressure can be applied to the body in many different ways that result in a chronic condition. For example, repeated contusions at a particular muscle site can produce a condition know as *myositis ossificans.* In its attempt to protect a chronically irritated bruise, the body reacts by creating a mineral deposit in the muscle. Myositis ossificans can cause a great deal of pain for the dancer and, if not properly resolved, may eventually require surgical removal. The dancer should note that any bruise that does not respond immediately to therapy should be referred to a physician for complete examination. Often the usual types of therapy such as ultrasound and massage only serve to irritate and increase the mineral deposits when myositis ossificans is present. X-ray examination will reveal mineral deposits 2 or 3 weeks after the initial injury.

Occasionally when a bruise has occurred to the soft musculature, a hematoma or blood tumor occurs within the muscle. A hematoma has a center of blood with an outer covering of thin connective tissue. A large hematoma often is not absorbed into the body spontaneously and consequently may have to be aspirated or evacuated medically by a hypodermic needle.

Compression injuries can occur chronically when improper postural alignment is present. This is particularly true in the feet. The dancer's feet normally undergo a great deal of stress, which is compounded by faulty dance technique or improper footwear. Generally speaking, shoes that are too narrow or too short cause the toes to be cramped, eventually resulting in toe deformity. The toe problems most prevalent in dancers are the bunion and the hammertoe. The bunion of the first or fifth metatarsal causes the great toe or the little toe to be forced toward the other toes. As a result, the joints become inflamed and often swollen from constant irritation. The hammertoe, in contrast, occurs as the result of the contraction of the toe flexor tendons and stretching of the toe

Table 2. Chronic compression condition management*

Common conditions	Basic signs	Management phase	Treatment program			
			Physical therapy	Dosage	Reconditioning	Dosage
Myositis ossificans	Ossification within a muscle caused by contusion that fails to respond to normal treatment and is marked by pain and swelling; x-ray examination may not show ossification until 2 or 3 weeks after injury	Symptomatic	1. Avoid massage 2. Apply superficial heat 3. Mild gradual stretch of part 4. Protective strapping or pad 5. Anti-inflammatory medication	Two or three times daily Two or three times daily As prescribed	1. Avoid all exercise that may irritate part 2. Gradual stretch	Two or three times daily
Myositis, fasciitis, and periostitis	Continuous low-grade inflammation in tissue with mild swelling and pain; often most severe following activity	Symptomatic	1. Application of superficial and deep heat 2. Ice massage 3. Protective strapping or padding 4. Anti-inflammatory medication	Two or three times daily Twice daily As prescribed	1. Rest part when possible 2. Gradual stretch of part following ice massage	Twice daily

*Adapted from Klafs, C. E., and Arnheim, D. D.: Modern principles of athletic training, ed. 3, St. Louis, 1973, The C. V. Mosby Co.

extensor tendons caused by shoes that are too short. Once developed, the hammertoe cannot be corrected by exercise or other positive means but can be relieved by strapping (Fig. 9-3). Bunions also produce inefficient movement and, if continually irritated, they eventually require surgery. Tape properly applied can help stablize a great toe that is developing a hallux valgus (Fig. 9-4).

The young dancer who goes on pointe before the feet are strong enough to maintain the foot, ankle, and leg in good alignment may develop deformities of the toes, particularly the great toe. The young child, therefore, should avoid going on pointe until the factors of weight, age, posture, and habits of body placement have been seriously considered.

Another problem unlike the bunion, although related, is the hallux rigidus. Although concerned with the great toe, the hallux rigidus is not a displacement like the bunion. The second joint of the great toe becomes extremely inflamed and painful in a straightened position and gradually over a long period of time becomes a permanently rigid toe.

Constant abnormal pressure on the feet can lead to the development of painful calluses and extra bone growths, or bone spurs. Constant pressure breaks down tissue and is eventually reflected in a chronic disabling problem. Feet, in

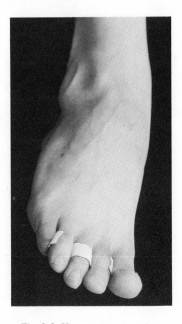

Fig. 9-3. Hammertoe strapping.

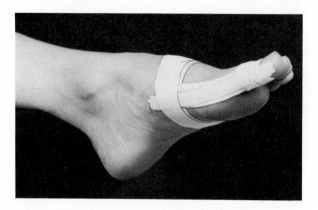

Fig. 9-4. Hallux valgus strapping.

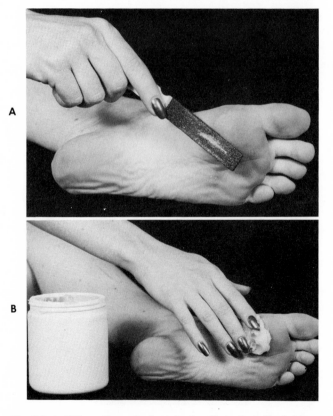

Fig. 9-5. A, Filing calluses. **B,** Applying lanolin to devitalized skin areas.

general, respond well to treatment of chronic inflammatory conditions by a regime of repeated soaks two or three times daily in water that is between 115° and 120° F. In situations where there is localized swelling and edema, contrast baths are effective.

Calluses

Dancers, since they are on their feet a great deal, cause the skin of the feet to shear against the supportive surface, producing calluses and/or blisters. Contrary to common thinking, callus is not a desirable condition for a foot to have. The cause of callus accumulation is often poor posture and weight bearing combined with faulty foot apparel. Callus accumulation reflects abnormal skin stresses and can result in an extremely painful condition of cracking and torn skin. A callus is tissue that is inelastic and has lost its viable yellow elastic tissue, which is normally present in the subdermal skin layer. Having lost this elasticity, the callus moves as a mass and is vulnerable to tears and fissures.

Proper foot hygiene helps to prevent callus formation. This is best accomplished by good dance technique, correct body alignment, the wearing of properly fitting footwear, and a good hygiene regime that is followed several times a week. After dance class or rehearsal it is desirable for the feet to be cleansed thoroughly, followed by a routine of filing off excess callus accumulation with an emery file and application of a very small amount of lanolin, which is massaged into the devitalized callus tissue (Fig. 9-5).

The dancer who senses abnormal friction on the foot should stop activity promptly and immediately give care to that area. Preventive care consists of eliminating irritation by friction-proofing the area. This can be done by rubbing it with petroleum jelly or padding it with a moleskin or tape covering that has been blanked out on the side that will lie next to the irritation. A strategically placed adhesive-backed pad can also help to take pressure off a painful callus (Fig. 9-6).

Friction blisters

Like calluses, friction blisters result from an excess of rubbing either within a shoe or as a result of skin rubbing against a nonyielding surface such as a stage or studio floor. Whatever the cause, the result of sustained friction is a separation of epidermis from the dermal skin layer with serum fluid accumulation under the epidermis. This fluid can be a clear serous material or can contain blood, depending on the depth of the tissues involved. The main concern of the dancer is to prevent blisters from occurring. This, like callus prevention, must be started when the skin is first irritated. At that time either a friction-proofing

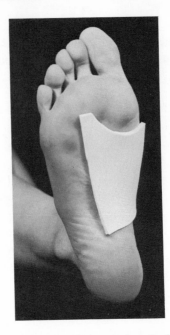

Fig. 9-6. Pad to relieve friction on the ball of the foot.

substance such as petroleum jelly or protection from a medium such as moleskin or a blanked-out piece of tape should cover the irritated area.

Once a blister has developed, the dancer then must prevent infection, but at the same time engage in full activity. Whenever possible the dancer with a blister should follow a conservative approach in its management to ensure that infection does not arise. If the blister is located in such a place on the foot that it could be easily irritated by additional friction, it is desirable to evacuate the fluid with a sterilized needle. Sterilization can be accomplished by burning the needle tip with a match and then cleaning the skin surface of the blister with rubbing alcohol. Following sterilization, the needle is introduced gently underneath the skin of the blister from about ⅛ inch outside the perimeter of the blister, tunneling under the blister until the fluid flows out. After evacuation, the blister should be protected by a felt or sponge rubber doughnut placed around the outside of the blister. Protected in this manner, the blister is allowed to heal. When it is no longer sensitive the skin may be cut away from the area and allowed to toughen naturally. The dancer should not handle a blood blister in this manner but should treat it by applying a doughnut and allowing the blister to reabsorb by itself. The reason for extreme care in cases of blood blisters is their predisposition to infection when additionally irritated.

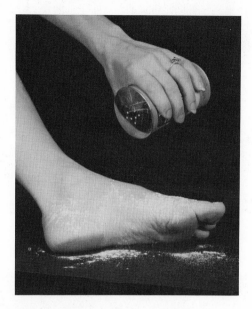

Fig. 9-7. Talcum powder helps to eliminate friction.

If any blister has been torn, it is desirable to cleanse the area thoroughly with an antiseptic such as Merthiolate and then pack it with a salve antiseptic such as zinc oxide. The skin flap is placed over the salve packing and a doughnut applied around its perimeter. When handled in this manner, the torn blister usually will not become contaminated because the salve provides protection from further infection and injury. In 2 or 3 days the skin can be cut away and the salve removed, allowing the new tender skin to be toughened.

If the dancer finds that the feet are extremely sensitive to irritation, it may be desirable to adopt a daily routine of applying benzoin followed by talcum powder (Fig. 9-7). The benzoin toughens the skin and eliminates the chances of friction injuries.

Corns

Corns are the result of abnormal pressure from improperly fitted shoes. They are of two types: hard corns (clavus durum) and soft corns (clavus molle). In both cases the pressures that come from the shoe cause the top tissue layer to be pressed inward, causing a corn-shaped growth to occur. Since it presses on nerve endings and causes inflammation, the corn can be extremely painful and handicapping. The hard corn is associated with hammertoe because of the skin

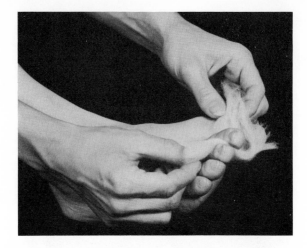

Fig. 9-8. Lamb's wool can often relieve the pain of a soft corn.

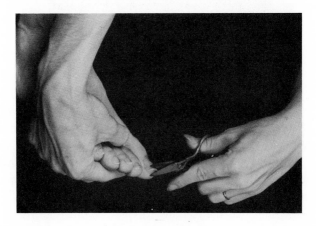

Fig. 9-9. Toenails should be trimmed straight across with a slight rounding on each end.

pressure of the toe against the top of the shoe. The soft corn is less serious than the hard corn and is usually found between the fourth and fifth toes. Painful hard corns must be referred to a specialist. However, the soft corn may be managed by some of the more common commercial medications on the market. Eliminating the basic cause often gives immediate relief. For example, flattening the hammertoe with a piece of tape may relieve the pain of the hard corn (Fig. 9-3), and the soft corn can be relieved by separating the toes with lamb's wool or cotton (Fig. 9-8).

Ingrown toenail

The ingrown toenail, like the other foot conditions discussed, can come from abnormal pressure from too short or too narrow shoes. Dancing on pointe may also cause this problem. Whatever the cause, the side edge of the toenail grows into the soft tissue of the skin, bringing about severe irritation and often infection. The ingrown toenail can be an extremely serious disabling condition and must be avoided. Avoidance is best accomplished by proper footwear and proper trimming of the toenails. The toenail should always be trimmed straight across with a slight rounding on each end (Fig. 9-9). The nail should never be rounded to the extent that it contacts the skin on either side of the nail bed.

If an ingrown toenail does occur, the foot should be soaked in 120° water two or three times daily, followed by the application of a thin wisp of cotton under the edge of the affected nail. This approach lifts the nail slightly from the nail bed, providing immediate relief from pain. This regime should be continued until the ingrown nail has grown out and symptoms are no longer present.

chapter ten

Strains

As discussed earlier, the abnormal pull of the musculotendinous unit is one of the dancer's most pressing problems. Fatigue, faulty body alignment, or improper dance technique can cause an overstretching or tearing of muscle fibers. The dancer usually experiences fatigue, spasm, and then the pain of stretching or tearing of the muscle. The onset of a strain can be prevented by stopping the activity at the point of fatigue. However, the sense of fatigue is often ignored with the mistaken idea that for progress to occur there must be discomfort in the body, or "if it hurts," that is good. This mistaken pain concept may eventually produce a chronic pathologic condition, incurring the risk of ruining a successful career. Another mistaken idea that many dancers have is that a part should be only stretched without the important back-up program of muscle strengthening. Overstretching the musculoskeletal unit often produces a lack of awareness of when a muscle has been lengthened too far. One must concur that stretching and full range of movement are necessary for success in dance; however, this should never be indulged in to the detriment of adequate muscle tone in a particular part.

Acute strains (Table 3)

The acute strain, like the contusion, is divided into first-, second-, and third-degree intensity. However, all strains should be treated as if they were one degree greater in intensity than they appear to be. The reader must be aware that it is difficult to specifically categorize an injury as to its exact intensity. There is a wide disparity in each degree of injury intensity. Therefore, if a dancer is in doubt about the intensity of an injury, it should be treated as if it were more severe than the symptoms dictate.

The symptoms of a first-degree strain can range from a very slight twinge in a muscle and soreness following activity to a local spasm with muscle weakness. There may even be some point tenderness in the area. Often the dancer is not aware that a mild strain has occurred and will not realize it until the next day when soreness is present. Most of the discomfort of the first-degree strain is due to muscle spasm and not to the tearing of muscle fibers. Therefore cold is applied to the area for 1 to 2 hours either by ice pack or by ice massage. If this is followed by a gradual stretch, much of the pain and discomfort can be eliminated. If soreness still persists after stretching, then a procedure of warm water soaks or warm (not to exceed 90° F.) whirlpool treatment may be initiated. A gradual stretching regime should be continued until soreness has completely subsided. In cases where soreness persists for more than 2 days, it is suggested that an elastic wrap be worn around the part to provide a mild external massage agent and at the same time provide some support to the injured muscle.

As in all cases of strain, the second-degree strain is caused by a hard sudden stretch of the musculotendinous unit that results in pain, a burning sensation, and a loss of function of that part for a short period of time. Spasm is usually associated with this problem as well as hemorrhaging and swelling. Swelling can be effectively controlled by a cold compress and elevation of the part immediately following the injury. Ideally, if a physician is immediately available, the dancer with a second-degree strain should be given medications that might include muscle relaxants and enzymes. If the loss of function lasts for more than ½ hour following proper immediate care, referral to a physician is routine. To most effectively assist nature in resolving the inflammatory process, it is suggested that the dancer apply cold compresses and elevate the part for at least 24 to 48 hours, depending on how quickly discomfort is overcome and function is returned. At no time should the dancer attempt to stretch out this condition because there is always torn tissue associated with the second-degree strain.

When the immediate phase of this injury has been resolved and hemorrhage appears to be under control, then a gradual warming process can begin first by whirlpool, if available, with a temperature of 90° for approximately 10 minutes or a heating pad set at warm, not hot, for approximately 20 minutes. An elastic wrap should be worn around the part to provide continual pressure and a soft tissue support, particularly when the dancer engages in physical activity. The

Table 3. Acute strain management*

Degree of injury	Basic signs	Treatment program				
		Management phase	Physical therapy	Dosage	Reconditioning	Dosage
First degree	Mild pull or stretch of musculotendinous unit causing spasm and sometimes pain and tenderness	Step 1: immediate care	1. Apply cold and pressure 2. Ice massage if spasm is present	½-2 hr. Daily	1. Gradual stretch following ice massage	Daily
Second degree	Moderate stretch and tear of portions of musculotendinous unit causing extreme spasm, point tenderness, loss of function, swelling, and discoloration	Step 1: immediate care	1. Apply cold and pressure; 20 min. on, 10 min. off 2. Elevation 3. Wear elastic wrap 4. Medication	24-48 hr. Up to 24 hr. As prescribed	1. Avoid exercise and stretch of part 2. General sustained exercise	Daily
		Step 2: second or third day	1. Gradual heating of part if hemorrhage has stopped; use superficial devices (soaks and pads at 105° F., whirlpool not to exceed 100° F. for 10 min.) 2. Massage above and below injury	Twice daily 5 min. twice daily	1. Avoid exercise and stretch of part 2. Continue general sustained exercise	Twice daily
		Step 3: third or fourth day	1. Continue superficial heat (soaks at 100° F., whirlpool at 105° F.) 2. Massage above and below injury 3. Analgesic balm 4. Elastic wrap	15 min. three times daily 5 min. three times daily When active When active	1. Avoid forced stretching of part 2. Start exercising part 3. Continue general sustained exercise	Daily Twice daily

	Step	Treatment	Frequency	Exercise program	Frequency
	Step 4: fourth or fifth day	1. Superficial heat	20 min. three times daily	1. Begin easy stretch of part (if pain free)	Daily
		2. Massage	Three times daily	2. Start program of PRE (progressive resistance exercise)	Twice daily
		3. Deep heat, if available	As prescribed	3. Continue program of general sustained exercise	Twice daily
		4. Analgesic balm	Symptomatic		
		5. Ice massage with gradual stretch	Daily		
		6. Elastic wrap	When active		
	Step 5	1. Therapy program is continued until dancer is symptom free	Three times daily	1. Continue until symptom free	Three times daily
Third degree		Severe muscle stretch causing extensive tissue tearing, rupture, or pulling away from bone			
	Step 1: immediate care	1. Refer to physician for x-ray examination and medication		1. Rest	48-72 hr.
		2. Apply cold and pressure; 20 min. on, 10 min. off	48-72 hr.		
		3. Elevation of part			
		4. Elastic wrap	24-48 hr.		
	Step 2: third or fourth day	1. Superficial heat (lukewarm)	10 min. twice daily	1. Avoid exercising and stretching part	
		2. Massage above and below injury	5 min. twice daily	2. Start general sustained exercise	Daily
		3. Elastic wrap			
	Step 3: fourth or fifth day	1. Superficial heart (warm)	Three times daily	1. Avoid exercising and stretching part	
		2. Massage above and below injury	Three times daily	2. General sustained exercise	Twice daily
		3. Analgesic balm packs	When active		
		4. Elastic wrap			

*Adapted from Klafs, C. E., and Arnheim, D. D.: Modern principles of athletic training, ed. 3, St. Louis, 1973, The C. V. Mosby Co.

Table 3. Acute strain management—cont'd

Degree of injury	Basic signs	Treatment program					
		Management phase	Physical therapy	Dosage	Reconditioning	Dosage
Third degree—cont'd		Step 4: fifth or sixth and following days	1. Superficial heat (regular temperatures)	20 min. three times daily	1. Begin easy stretching of part if pain free	Daily
			2. Massage	5 min. three times daily	2. Start PRE	Twice daily
			3. Deep heat	As prescribed	3. Continue general sustained exercise	Twice daily
			4. Analgesic balm	When active		
			5. Elastic wrap			
		Step 5	1. Therapy program is continued until dancer is symptom free	Three times daily	1. Continue until symptom free	Three times daily

dancer should gradually increase the temperature of the whirlpool or immersion baths until the maximum is reached in 4 to 5 days. The dancer should begin a general exercise or activities program that excludes the affected part. Specific exercise of the affected part should start when there is no discomfort on movement. At no time should the dancer attempt stretching the moderate strain if pain is present. A program of specific therapeutic exercise can be instituted along with flexibility exercises when the injury is symptom free.

The third-degree strain is the most severe of all strains and when it is incurred the dancer must be immediately referred to a physician for treatment. Determination is best made by how much function is lost in the strained part. Typically the dancer will complain of a sudden snap or tear and a burning sensation in the affected part along with spasm, point tenderness, and inability to contract the muscle. If the strain was sustained at the muscle origin, or insertion, then the dancer should suspect the possibility of the muscle having torn away from the bone. If the injury occurs to the soft belly portion of the muscle, then the possibility of muscle rupture should be entertained. In any case the severe strain demands immediate referral to a physician for x-ray examination and medication. The immediate care of cold, pressure, and elevation is carried out for as long as 72 hours, while gradual heating is not usually begun for about 3 or 4 days after the initial injury has occurred.

After the immediate care phase, the dancer should engage in a general exercise program while avoiding movements that may aggravate the injury. As indicated earlier, the generalized exercise program encourages the healing process, and there should be a decrease in the amount of scar tissue at the strain site. The elastic wrap should be kept on the affected part while the dancer is active or until the part is symptom free. Specific progressive exercise is not given to the affected part until about 5 days to a week following the initial injury episode, at which time a gradual program of strengthening and flexibility is started. The dancer should avoid being in too much of a hurry to return to full activity. Attempting to force an injury to heal before nature has intended or engaging in activity before the injury has become resolved often produces a subacute or chronic condition. This is particularly true when there has been an overstretching of a tendon. A dancer should allow the body to heal the injury in its own time. To be in too much of a hurry causes scarring and increases the susceptibility to a recurrence of the same injury.

Cramps or muscle spasms

Muscle spasms have been discussed throughout this book as being associated with any compression or stretching of soft tissue. Although not always obvious to the dancer, the muscle cramp is also a muscle spasm. However, the cramp may be considered a sudden violent and involuntary contraction of the muscle that is immediately painful. Muscle cramping can either be the clonic or tonic type. The clonic cramp is identified by intermittent contractions and relaxation of the muscle, pulsating almost like a heartbeat, while the tonic type is a steady or constant contraction of a particular muscle. The direct cause of the cramp is difficult to pinpoint, but fatigue, fluid and mineral depletion through excessive perspiration, and breaking down the reciprocal muscle coordination are major causative factors. Sometimes the cramp occurs during some activity and at other times it occurs when the dancer is at rest or asleep.

At no time when a cramp occurs should the dancer attempt to dance through the problem, but should stop immediately and attempt to reduce the cramp. Initially a cramp should not be massaged but should be grasped firmly, applying constant pressure until it subsides. When the cramp has melted away, mild gradual stretch can be applied to the area, followed by a more vigorous stretch when the cramp is completely under control. After stretching, the cramp can be treated by application of superficial heat or analgesic balm. If the dancer has cramps daily in different areas of the body, referral to a physician is necessary. The physician may prescribe salt and/or calcium supplementation as a possible approach to alleviating the problem.

Foot and ankle strains

Strains about the foot are common in dance and occur often to the toes, the arch, or the ankle region. Foot and ankle strains often come from dancing on very hard unyielding surfaces. The toe most often strained is the great toe, which is primarily used in propelling the dancer in leaps and landings. Often associated with foot and ankle strain is faulty foot alignment such as seen in dancers with extremely high or low longitudinal arches. The arch strain will be discussed more fully in Chapter 11.

Following the acute stage of the toe strain or the arch strain the dancer should begin a program of preventive exercising (Fig. 10-1). Also, to assist the healing process and to prevent additional trauma to the strained arch, strapping should be used routinely when the dancer is active. The dancer can elect to use one of three strapping techniques that will provide moderate support until the arch tendons have recovered from strain.

Technique A: simple arch strapping with pad (Fig. 10-2, *A*). The dancer with mild pain and general discomfort in the various foot tendons can find relief by applying two or three strips of 1½-inch linen-backed tape or two strips of 2-inch elastic tape around the arch. However, a more substantial technique is to

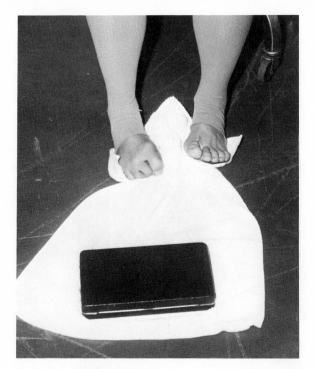

Fig. 10-1. Toes and arch exercise. Placing a book or light weight on a towel, the dancer gathers the material to a mound by gripping with the toes.

incorporate, a sponge rubber pad along the longitudinal arch area, combining it with circles of tape. The pad is made of ¼-inch sponge rubber cut to the shape of the individual arch.

Technique B: arch X *strapping* (Fig. 10-2, *B*). This technique is designed to provide some support for the longitudinal arch and is particularly valuable in cases of arch strain or the beginning of a fallen arch. The procedure is to first apply a 1-inch circle of tape around the ball of the foot to act as an anchor for the major support tape. The tape starts from the metatarsophalangeal joint of the great toe, crosses the center of the arch, goes around the heel, and back across the center of the arch, ending at the metatarsophalangeal joint on the little toe side. This procedure is repeated once more and is then locked in place by circles of tape placed around the ball and arch. If possible, the technique should be finished with 2-inch elastic tape.

Technique C: single or double cross arch strapping (Fig. 10-2, *C*). This technique is designed for the more severely strained arch and also can be used for re-aligning a twisted forefoot. As in technique B, the circle of tape is placed around

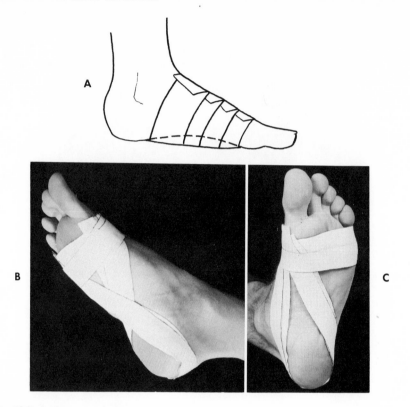

Fig. 10-2. Arch support techniques. **A,** Simple arch strapping with pad. **B,** Arch X strapping. **C,** Single cross arch strapping.

the metatarsophalangeal joint loosely to act as an anchor for the arch tape strips. Starting on either side of the foot, a strip of 1-inch tape is run from the metatarsophalangeal joint straight along the side of the foot, around the heel, crossing the center of the arch and ending at the point where the tape began. The technique is repeated on the other side of the foot. Both procedures are repeated again until two strips of tape have been applied to each side of the foot.

ACHILLES TENDON STRAIN. Strain of the Achilles tendon is also frequent in dance and is caused by a sudden overstretching of the Achilles tendon caused by a forcible pushing of the foot against the floor. In this situation the Achilles tendon is stretched and then contracts suddenly, which causes a tissue tear. This problem should be immediately treated and protected against another injury because the Achilles tendon tends to develop a chronic condition following acute strain episodes. (See Achilles tenosynovitis, p. 142.)

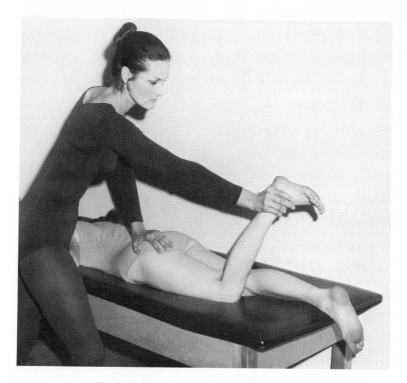

Fig. 10-3. Strengthening the hamstring muscles.

Leg strains

HAMSTRING STRAIN. Hamstring strains have a high incidence in most physically active persons who use their legs extensively. The reason for this high incidence is difficult to determine. In dance the hamstring group is often extensively stretched without a protective strengthening program (Fig. 10-3). An imbalance in the strength of the quadriceps muscle in front of the thigh and the hamstring group in back of the thigh predisposes the hamstring to spasm, fatigue, and subsequent strain. Susceptibility to hamstring strain is also prevalent in those persons who have a strength difference of more than 10% between the left and right hamstring group and those in whom a hamstring group has 50% less strength than the opposing quadriceps muscle group.

When it comes to conditioning and injury prevention, one must consider the hamstrings as the most neglected muscle group in the body. Therefore the dancer should include leg flexion and hip extension movements (for example,

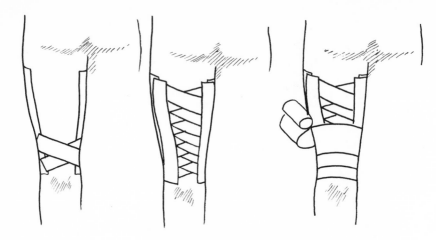

Fig. 10-4. Hamstring X strapping.

passé to attitude to arabesque) in the conditioning program whenever possible. The hamstring strain is often obvious to the dancer before it occurs. Fatigue is the first and most obvious sign; it is followed by spasm and then the actual stretching and tearing of muscle tissue. If the hamstring area feels tired or "dead," the dancer should avoid all stretching and dance activities that may overly stress this area and should immediately engage in a gradual strengthening program.

Treatment of the hamstring strain is in keeping with care of any typical strain. However, the dancer should be encouraged to engage in a general movement program as soon as possible. It is desirable that the general exercise program consist of many locomotor activities that do not overly fatigue or stretch the hamstring muscles. For protection the dancer should wear an elastic wrap around the thigh. The elastic wrap provides a mild support to the muscles and helps to prevent overstretching and aggravation of the area. If the dancer must engage in vigorous activity even though the hamstring strain has not completely recovered, a tape support can be utilized.

Hamstring strapping (Fig. 10-4). Both the hamstring and the quadriceps muscle groups can be protected by X strapping. This technique is designed to support muscles against gravity and to provide external soft compression. The materials for the hamstring X technique can either be 1½- or 2-inch linen tape or, ideally, 2- or 3-inch elastic tape. The hamstring technique is started by a strip of tape between 6 and 9 inches long on each side of the thigh. With the lower leg slightly bent to relax the hamstring muscles, the tape is crisscrossed starting just above the bend of the knee and working upward to the base of the buttock. When the crisscrossing has been completed, strips of tape are applied on both sides of the thigh to hold the X's in place. Finally, elastic wrap is applied to the thigh to prevent the tape from becoming loose during activity.

QUADRICEPS STRAIN. In active males the quadriceps muscle is less often strained than the hamstring group; however, this is not the case in the female dancer. The reason may be the difference between female and male in the line of muscle pull resulting from the female's slightly wider pelvis. Unlike the hamstring strain, which often occurs from a sudden abnormal stretch, the quadriceps strain occurs primarily from a static muscle contraction. For example, the dancer places the quadriceps muscle in stretch by bending the knee about 40 degrees and then attempts to hold this position, exerting a stress on the full length of the muscle. Like the hamstring strain, the quadriceps strain can be protected from repeated trauma by the application of a tape or elastic wrap support. It should also be noted that jumping, landing, and locking the knees suddenly cause a common dance problem in which the patellar tendon is repeatedly pulled, resulting in a tibial tendinitis. Additional discussion of the quadriceps strain will be presented in the section on chronic strains.

Hip strain

Crossing the hip joint are a great many muscles and tendons that allow the thigh full mobility. The dancer places great demands on the full mobility of the hip, frequently overstretching the muscles and supportive tissue in that area. The groin, which is the region lying between the thigh and the abdomen, is one of the most often strained areas in dance. The muscles in the area of the groin primarily allow the dancer to flex, adduct, and inwardly rotate the thigh. These actions are produced by the iliopsoas, the rectus femoris, and the adductor muscle groups. Like many other muscles and groups of muscles that are susceptible to strain, the groin muscles are commonly overstretched by the dancer who is already very loose jointed (by floor stretches in stride) but has not given thought to increasing strength proportionally to the gain in joint flexibility. As a result, groin muscles often fail to acquire enough muscle tone to prevent the hip from becoming suddenly overstretched. The dancer who suddenly twists, internally rotating the thigh or trunk, may incur a groin strain.

Because of the complexity of the muscles in the hip region, it is important to the dancer to know whether the strain is accessible to topical therapy or whether it is deep, requiring more definitive professional care. The less serious strain can be dealt with nicely by cold and superficial heat, but the deep strain is not readily amenable to any physical therapy approach and is usually self-limiting. The self-limiting injury is one in which therapy does little good.

Fig. 10-5. Leg extension against resistance to test for strain of rectus femoris muscle.

To determine the seriousness of a groin strain it is advisable that a functional test be given. The first test is for the rectus femoris, the only two-joint muscle of the quadriceps group (Fig. 10-5). This relatively superficial muscle, besides extending the knee, crosses the hip joint and assists the dancer in flexing the thigh or bending the trunk forward. To test this muscle, the dancer sits on a table with both legs hanging over the end. While the dancer extends the affected leg, gradual resistance is applied until it is fully extended. This application of resistance puts stress specifically on the rectus femoris muscle, and if a strain is present, pain will be felt in the groin area.

A second test for a fairly superficial muscle group is the thigh adductor test (Fig. 10-6). In this test the dancer lies on the table with the affected leg abducted as wide as possible. The leg is then pulled to the midline position against resistance. If pain is felt on this movement, then it is assumed that one of the adductor muscles is strained.

The third test, which is designed to reflect strain in the deep iliopsoas muscle of the hip, requires the dancer to sit on the edge of the table with both legs

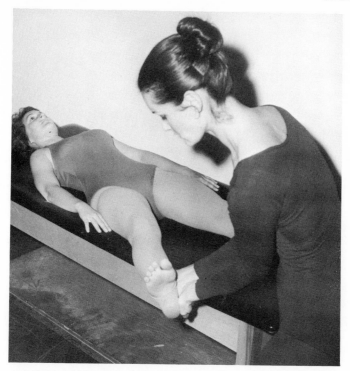

Fig. 10-6. Pressing thigh inward toward the midline against resistance to test for a strain of the adductor muscles.

hanging over the end. The dancer then lifts the affected thigh upward against a resistance. A strain of the iliopsoas would be identified by a deep pain in the groin area. Hopefully the dancer does not strain this very deep and important muscle. Without the full function of the iliopsoas, the dancer is unable to efficiently maintain an upright posture and to move the thigh effectively. The treatment of the groin strain should be conservative, including the avoidance of physical activity as long as possible and engaging in such physical therapy as whirlpool, hot packs, and in case of deeper injuries, diathermy and ultrasound therapy. If exercise must be engaged in, the dancer should wear a groin support wrap to decrease the possibilities of overstretching.

Groin wrap (Fig. 10-7). The groin wrap is a spica bandage applied in a specific manner to help the dancer decrease the chances of reinjury. A 4- or 6-inch elastic wrap is used. The dancer stands with the affected thigh turned inward. The wrap is started at the upper end of the inner side of the thigh, carried to the inside, then around the outside and over the crest of the ilium in front of the abdomen. It is then carried around the back and the same

Fig. 10-7. Groin wrap.

pattern is retraced until all the material is applied. If additional support is needed, a pad should be placed on the strained site for additional compression. To ensure greater stability, elastic tape could also be applied by tracing the pattern of the wrap.

Back and neck strain

The spine is an area of the body that is extremely vulnerable to strain in dance. Exceeding the particular individual limits of the back often results in muscular strain and, more seriously, in a sprain. The spine allows a great variety of movements. For example, flexion is allowed in the neck, or cervical region, and the upper thoracic, lumbar, and lumbosacral regions. Hyperextension of the back is mainly prevented in the thoracic vertebrae by the protruding spinal processes. Side bending, or lateral flexion, occurs in the cervical area and in a somewhat limited degree in the lumbar area. Rotation occurs freely in the neck as a result of the lack of heavy, bony, interlocking articular processes of the cervical vertebrae.

Many factors make the back and neck prone to injury. The most common of these factors are due to the great diversity in how backs are anatomically formed. Posture, body alignment, and the dancer's attempt to exceed the basic structural or anatomical limitations of the spine may result in serious injury. It is commonly accepted that the human spine is in the process of evolutionary change and that many individuals have spines that are abnormal. For example, many individuals have four or even six lumbar vertebrae instead of five. Likewise many individuals have six or eight cervical vertebrae instead of the customary seven. Some individuals have extra ribs and other types of structural anomalies of the vertebrae that, when overstressed by physical activity, may result in serious pathologic conditions.

Strains of the back and neck usually come as a result of sudden uncommon movements such as rotation or hyperextension resulting from improper warm-up. The neck is particularly vulnerable to muscular strain because it is not usually well conditioned and is weaker as compared to most other areas of the dancer's body. Moving the head suddenly in a snapping fashion can easily result in whiplash neck strain. A sudden forward or backward movement of the trunk can produce spasm strain with severe handicapping pain. Susceptibility to low back strain is increased by the postural problem of lordosis with its associated tight low back and weak abdominal musculature.

Sudden acute injury to the neck and back region should be treated like any typical strain. However, because of the back's propensity to muscle spasm rather than tearing of muscle tissue, the practice of ice massage combined with a gradual stretch often relieves the symptoms almost instantaneously. This is particularly true in the cervical, upper back, and lumbar regions. Dancers with injuries to the back and neck that do not respond to palliative treatment within a week should be routinely referred to a physician. The male dancer is particularly susceptible to back strain when he is executing a lift improperly.

Arm and shoulder strain

In dancers the incidence of arm strain is not as high as the incidence of strain of the lower limbs. There are occasions, however, when the dancer strains muscles in the arm or shoulder because of a fall on an outstretched arm, a sudden twist, or lifting of a heavy load. The shoulder's basic design is for full mobility; hence it is seldom strained in dance except in a situation where there is extreme rotation, such as falling on the arm in an awkward position or lifting a partner when off balance. This causes strain of the small intrinsic muscles of the shoulder that cause inward and outward rotation. The dancer who is unable to internally or externally rotate the shoulder without pain or who is unable to raise the arm out to the side may be considered to have strained the deeper muscles of the shoulder such as the rotator cuff. Topical therapy to the shoulder is not usually effective, but moist heat does have some palliative effect in relaxation of the overly tense muscles. Often the therapy of choice in injuries to the shoulder is ultrasound or diathermy. The most important concern in managing a strained shoulder is to overcome the problem of immobility, which often results in muscle contractures together with a severe loss of movement. It is important that the dancer try to maintain a normal range of shoulder movement without aggravating the condition. This means that, in the early stages of injury, rotation of the shoulder should be maintained by nongravity-type exercises. For example, the affected arm is rotated while it is allowed to hang down in a relaxed manner.

When the dancer is pain free and able to initiate a regular exercise program, the concern should be full range activities in the upright posture. Progressive resistance exercises of the shoulder should not be initiated until the dancer can easily execute free shoulder movements while standing in the upright posture.

The elbow and wrist have a lower incidence of injury in dance than does the shoulder. Normally the elbow is strong and can withstand the many rigors placed on it; in contrast, the wrist is more vulnerable to injury, mainly in attempting to brace the body in a fall. As in reconditioning of the shoulder, one should first be concerned with maintaining the range of movement in the elbow. However, the elbow must never be forced to regain its flexibility, but should be allowed to do so gradually. This is because the injured elbow tends to rapidly develop contractures and scar tissue when placed into a forced program of reconditioning. The wrist injury, specifically the sprain, will be discussed in Chapter 11.

Chronic strains (Table 4)

The chronic strain comes about from many acute episodes that can result in conditions such as myositis, fasciitis, or tenosynovitis, depending on the particular injury site. As with other chronic conditions, the chronic strain represents a constantly irritated area that has developed a tension within the tissues that the body is unable to overcome. Dancers, because of their desire for perfection and their fear that if they miss a class their technique will deteriorate, often place themselves in a situation where a chronic strain is inevitable. If the acute single strain episode were properly cared for, the chronic problem would not occur.

Fallen arch

The fallen arch is attributed to the chronically stretched tendons and ligaments of the foot. Once fallen, the arch cannot be restored. Consequently, prevention of the initial problem or preventing further falling is of major concern to the dancer. To prevent the arch from dropping, a daily routine of foot exercises should be undertaken, along with avoidance of activities that put a great deal of abnormal strain on the foot, such as dancing on hard, nonresilient surfaces. Sore arches will benefit from therapy procedures such as hot water soaks at 110° to 120° F. several times daily combined with supportive taping.

Achilles tenosynovitis

As discussed on p. 134, the Achilles tendon is highly susceptible to strain. Repeated strain to this area results in a condition known as tenosynovitis, in which the synovial sheath that covers and lubricates the tendon becomes

Table 4. Chronic strain management*

Common conditions	Basic signs	Management phase	Treatment program			
			Physical therapy	Dosage	Reconditioning	Dosage
Simple muscle soreness	Mild to moderate muscle tenderness on palpation and movement	Symptomatic	1. Ice massage followed by gradual stretch	Two to three times daily	1. Gradual stretching	Two to three times daily
Tendinitis, tenosynovitis, myositis, fasciitis, and bursitis	Continuous low-grade inflammation with pain on movement, local weakness with restriction on muscle stretching, and point tenderness	Symptomatic	1. Superficial heat 2. Ice massage after stretch 3. Deep heat 4. Anti-inflammatory drugs	Three times daily Two to three times daily As prescribed As prescribed	1. Rest 2. Gradual stretching	Two to three times daily

*Adapted from Klafs, C. E., and Arnheim, D. D.: Modern principles of athletic training, ed. 3, St. Louis, 1973, The C. V. Mosby Co.

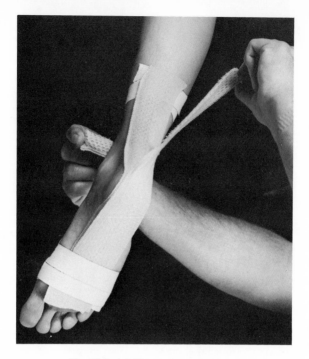

Fig. 10-8. Achilles tendon strapping.

chronically inflamed. Tenosynovitis can be further categorized as the dry or wet type. The dry type means that the lubricating fluid of the synovial membrane is not present; consequently, the dancer complains of a rubbing or grating sound when the tendon is moved. The wet type indicates an overproduction of lubricant due to chronic irritation of the synovial membrane that produces a swelling and painful pressure. Because the Achilles tendon is involved in almost all foot movement, it is extremely difficult to prevent further irritation once an injury has been incurred. Another problem that is associated with the overstretching of the Achilles tendon is an inflammation of the bursa that is present where the Achilles tendon joins the calcaneus. This bursa can also be irritated by the constant pressure of dance shoes, producing symptoms similar to those of the strained Achilles tendon.

The dancer with these problems should make every effort to avoid irritating activity and to shorten the Achilles tendon by raising the heel with a customized pad. When street shoes are worn, a ¼-inch sponge rubber pad placed under each heel will help to alleviate some of the irritation. If dancing must be engaged in, then Achilles tendon strapping should be applied.

Achilles tendon strapping (Fig. 10-8). The technique for Achilles tendon strapping utilizes 2- or 3-inch elastic tape and 1-inch linen tape. The foot should be relaxed completely with two 1-inch anchor strips applied around the ball of the foot and lower leg approximately 4 to 5 inches above the malleolus (ankle bone). One strip of elastic tape is then placed starting at the ball of the foot, stretched across the bottom of the foot and up the back of the heel, and joined to the anchor strip around the leg. This first elastic tape strip should be stretched firmly, but not to the full extent of the tape. A second strip is applied over the first but is cut approximately 4 inches longer. The upper end of the second strip is cut and split lengthwise, with each separate strip wrapped around the lower leg, forming a lock. This technique is completed by two or three anchor strips wrapped around the foot and the lower leg. The Achilles tendon strapping still allows the dancer to move but prevents the Achilles tendon from being overstretched.

Shin splints

Shin splints is one of the most common problems that plague dancers. It is characterized by leg pain and irritation, which become increasingly more tender and sore after vigorous activity has ceased. The specific site of shin splints is often vague but is commonly thought to be the posterior or anterior tibial muscles or the interossei muscles between the tibia and fibula. It is best characterized by a dull ache in the lower shin area. This condition most often occurs during the very early conditioning period of new classes, indicating inadequate fitness, and again toward the end of classes, which would indicate fatigue. It often occurs when dancing on very hard nonyielding surfaces for long periods of time. Other factors that seem to increase the incidence of this problem are an imbalance in leg length and arch problems. Because of the great diversity of possible causes, one can deduce that shin splints are caused mainly by a lack of reciprocal coordination between opposing muscles of the lower leg resulting from one muscle pulling against another. The cause of shin splints may be present alone or in combination with two or even three other conditions; therefore it is difficult to pinpoint the exact reason why a dancer develops this problem. Once dancers contract shin splints, susceptibility is greater in the future.

The treatment of shin splints is usually symptomatic, with the most beneficial approach being the continual application of superficial heat over a long period of time. Whirlpool at 105° F. or hot water soaks at 120° F. and the application of analgesic balm packs have been found to be the most effective treatment procedures. Such physical therapy modalities as diathermy and

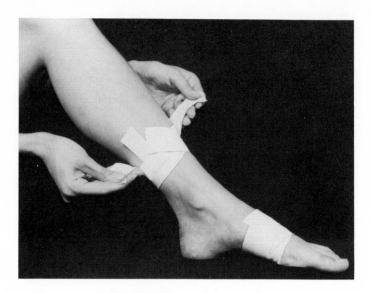

Fig. 10-9. Shin splints strapping.

ultrasound therapy have not proved themselves to be any more beneficial to the dancer than this less expensive superficial approach. Along with the superficial heat treatment, the dancer should engage in a stretch routine that includes stretching of the anterior and posterior muscles both before and after activity. This is extremely important. (See Figs. 4-6 and 4-7 for effective shin splints stretches.) Also, those dancers who have a history of shin splints should make this stretch routine a preventive procedure. In order for a dancer to continue activity a strapping technique should be used that will alleviate some of the pain and discomfort.

Shin splints strapping (Fig. 10-9). While the dancer is in a seated position, the affected leg is bent, causing the lower leg muscles to be relaxed and soft to the touch. In this leg position a 1-inch by 2-inch strip of foam rubber or adhesive felt is applied directly over the sore area. A series of circular strips of either 1½-inch linen or 2-inch elastic tape is applied around the leg, starting below the irritation and working upward. Each strip of tape should start from the back and be brought around the front, drawing the muscle tissue to the bone. It is also advantageous to apply either the figure-of-eight or the X arch strapping around the longitudinal arch of the foot. A dancer with shin splints that is not resolved in 2 or 3 weeks should be automatically referred to a physician because of the possibility of stress fracture in this area.

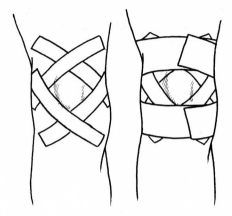

Fig. 10-10. Patella strapping.

Patellar tendinitis

The patellar tendon strain is a condition that is increasing in incidence in the dance field mainly because of the types of static quadriceps contraction activities that are currently practiced, for example, holding a position on half toe with knees bent and the body inclined back. This problem, much like Achilles tendinitis, becomes chronic following just a few acute episodes. The dancer who complains of a constant pain and mild swelling in the area around the patella and is free from bone spurs or degeneration of the patella most likely will be diagnosed as having patellar tendinitis.

Ideally, the dancer with this problem should place the quadriceps muscle at complete rest. If rest is not possible, a therapeutic program of superficial heat and support might prevent further injury. Ultrasound therapy has also been found to be beneficial to chronic problems in this area. A tape support with a spiral elastic wrap often assists the dancer in not exceeding the limits imposed by this problem (Fig. 10-10). Both ice massage and static stretch have been found to be beneficial in decreasing swelling in some cases. Activities that involve violent static contraction of the quadriceps muscle must be avoided at all costs; however, a slow gradual stretch routine should be initiated before and after an activity session.

"The clicks" (joint noises)

Many dancers complain that when they move their joints make strange noises similar to clicks, crunches, or thumps. The causes of joint noises are varied.

Often the dancer stretches tendons that cross joints to the point that they respond by snapping across the joint when the part is stretched or moved in a certain way. In most cases the snapping tendon, if not associated with pain, is not considered harmful but the dancer should not be encouraged to snap a tendon continually because it may eventually develop into a chronic problem. Also, joint noises can be elicited from a capsule surrounding a joint that becomes slack from continually exceeding anatomically normal limits or from within a joint, as in the case of clicks or creaking noises.

chapter eleven

Sprains, dislocations, and fractures

Although less common than injuries to the musculotendinous unit, injuries to the joint and bone do happen in dance. Sprains, dislocations, and even fractures can result from the rigors of dance.

Sprains (Table 5)

The most common sprains occurring to the dancer are sprains to the toes, ankles, knees, hip, low back, and occasionally the wrists. As discussed earlier, the sprain is primarily an injury to the ligamentous supportive structures of a joint. However, because tendons cross joints, a sprain can also adversely affect tendons. Like contusions and strains, the sprain is categorized into first, second, and third degrees of intensity. The intensity of a sprain is best determined by the extent of the dancer's disability as well as the tenderness elicited by feel or palpation and the amount of hemorrhage and swelling present. Unlike the dancer with a strain or contusion, a dancer with a second- or third-degree sprain must routinely be referred to a physician for x-ray examination and diagnosis. This is because fracture is commonly associated with a twisted joint. A joint that has

Table 5. Acute sprain management*

Degree of injury	Basic signs	Management phase	Treatment program			
			Physical therapy	Dosage	Reconditioning	Dosage
First degree	Mild twist of joint causing a twinge of discomfort produced by minimal hemorrhage	Step 1: immediate care	1. Apply cold and pressure; 20 min. on, 10 min. off 2. Elevation 3. Tape or wrap support for continual pressure	1-2 hr. 1 hr. Variable	1. Avoid moving joint 2. General sustained exercise	Daily Daily
		Step 2: second day	1. Superficial heat 2. Massage above and below injury 3. Wrap if swelling is present	10 min. one to two times daily 5 min. one to two times daily	1. Move joint to retain range of movement	One to two times daily
Second degree	Moderate twist of joint resulting in pain, loss of function for several minutes or longer, and point tenderness; swelling occurs if proper immediate care is not given	Step 1: immediate care	1. Apply cold and pressure; 20 min. on, 10 min. off 2. Elevation 3. Apply tape or wrap for continual pressure 4. Referral to physician for x-ray examination	24-48 hr. 24 hr. 24 hr.	1. No weight bearing if ankle or knee 2. Crutch walking 3. General sustained exercise	3 days Daily
		Step 2: second or third day	1. Superficial heat (90°) 2. Massage above and below injury 3. Continue wrap for pressure	10 min. twice daily 5 min. twice daily	1. No weight bearing if ankle or knee 2. Continue crutch walking 3. Move part for range of movement 4. General sustained exercise	Twice daily Daily

	Step	Treatment		Exercise	
	Step 3: third or fourth day	1. Superficial heat (warm) or contrast baths if swelling is present	Three times daily	1. ...weight bearing with support	
		2. Massage of part	Three times daily	2. Move part for range of movement	
		3. Analgesic balm packs when generally active	Twice daily	3. General sustained exercise	Twice daily
	Step 4	1. Therapy program is continued until dancer is symptom free	Daily	1. Continue until symptom free	Daily
Third degree	Severe joint twist causing extreme pain, loss of function over long period, point tenderness, and usually immediate swelling with later discoloration	Step 1: immediate care			
		1. Cold and pressure	48-72 hr.	1. No weight bearing if ankle or knee	
		2. Elevation	24-48 hr.	2. Crutch walking	
		3. Tape or wrap for constant pressure and stabilization		3. Rest part	3-5 days
		4. Refer to physician for x-ray examination and medication	As prescribed		
	Step 2: third or fourth day	1. Superficial heat (warm)	15 min. twice daily	1. No weight bearing	
		2. Massage above and below injury	5 min. twice daily	2. Crutch walking	
		3. Maintain tape or wrap for constant pressure		3. Move part for range of movement	Twice daily
				4. General sustained exercise	Twice daily
	Step 3: fourth or fifth day	1. Superficial heat or contrast bath if swelling persists	Three times daily	1. Weight bearing if no limp	
		2. Massage	Three times daily	2. Move part to restore range of movement	Twice daily
		3. Analgesic balm pack when active		3. General sustained exercise	Twice daily
	Step 4	1. Therapy program is continued until dancer is symptom free; support may be required	Daily	1. Continue until symptom free	Daily

*Adapted from Klafs, C. E., and Arnheim, D. D.: Modern principles of athletic training, ed. 3, St. Louis, 1973, The C. V. Mosby Co.

lost its ability to function for more than several minutes must be considered to have either a second- or third-degree sprain. Ice, pressure, and elevation should be routinely employed to control hemorrhage and swelling in the joint. This procedure is even more important for joint injury than in cases of injury to a muscle because injured joints rapidly swell with the effusion of blood and serum. A second- or third-degree sprain may demand joint immobilization to ensure a speedy recovery. However, each type of joint injury has its own characteristics in terms of therapeutic requirements.

Toe sprains

The barefoot dancer has a high incidence of stubbed toes, particularly the great toe. Jamming against an immovable object or suddenly twisting the great toe are hazards of the dance profession. Usually a sprained toe responds positively to application of the procedures shown in Table 5. However, there may be no weight bearing allowed for a period of time and/or a special strapping may be necessary to provide stability. If the sprain has occurred to toes other than the great toe, then the best immobilization procedure is that in which the affected toe is taped to an adjacent unaffected toe.

Great toe strapping (Fig. 11-1). Strapping the great toe can be initiated by using a combination of 1- and ½-inch tape. Starting the ½-inch tape from the middle of the foot, the tape is carried from the great toe to the first toe, encircling it and then coming over its top and returning to the starting point. Two or three tape strips can be applied with their ends anchored by 1-inch tape strip encircling the metatarsophalangeal joint. This tape technique supports the second joint of the great toe and the ball of the foot.

Ankle sprain

When considering a sprain, one usually thinks of the ankle joint (Fig. 11-2). Even though structurally the ankle may be considered a moderately strong joint, it is subject to sudden twists, especially when the dancer steps on some irregular surface. The highest incidence of injury is to the outside aspect of the ankle. This occurs when the dancer turns the foot inward, placing an abnormal stretch on the outer ankle ligaments. Usually a dancer has a high level of flexibility in the ankle region, and it takes a great deal of force to actually cause a sprain. If this force is great enough, ligaments will be torn and even a part of the outer ankle bone may be pulled away. Also, the center talus bone may roll underneath and strike against the internal ankle bone, causing a fracture on the inside of the ankle.

Inability to bear weight on the affected foot and rapid swelling must be

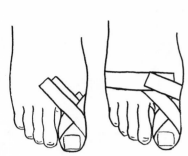

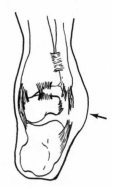

Fig. 11-1. Sprained toe strapping. **Fig. 11-2.** Lateral (outside) ankle sprain.

considered symptoms of fracture and a physician should be consulted immediately. Some physicians may routinely apply a cast to a second- or third-degree sprain as well as a fracture for a week or longer to ensure proper repair. On the other hand, some physicians will apply a tape support to the sprain and instruct the dancer to engage in no weight bearing for 2 or 3 days, followed by a program of physical therapy.

The medial sprain presents a different problem than the lateral sprain because even though it occurs less frequently it is much more serious than a lateral ankle sprain. This is because injuring the inside ligaments also affects the inner longitudinal arch. Often dancers who have had medial sprains experience arch difficulties. It is suggested that, along with regular rehabilitation regimes, the dancer with inside sprain engage in a program of arch and foot reconditioning. As in all sprains, once the ligaments of the ankle have been stretched, exercise cannot restore joint stability. Therefore strapping is the best preventive procedure.

Ankle strapping technique (Fig. 11-3). The purpose of the ankle strapping technique is to provide mild support to the ankle joint and still allow for foot and ankle mobility. The main materials required are 1- and ½-inch tape and tape adherent. Maintaining the foot in a neutral (90-degree) position, the dancer places one anchor strip about 4 inches above the malleolus and then applies two stirrups along the side of the ankle, starting just in front of the Achilles tendon and overlapping each piece of tape approximately one half the width of the preceding piece. Once the stirrups are in place, circle strips are applied around the lower leg and down past the malleolus, locking the stirrups in place and providing a mild support to the lower leg tendons. Next, two arch strips and a heel lock are applied. The heel lock is applied by starting the tape high on

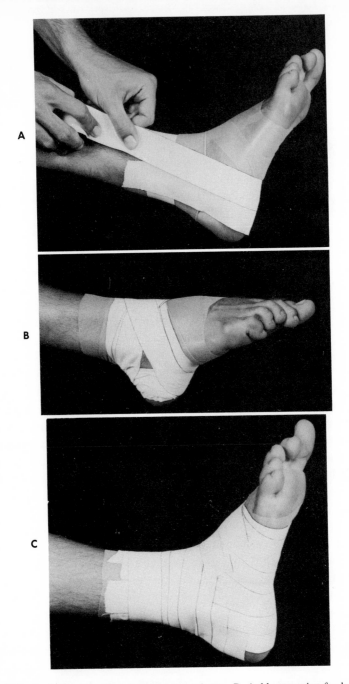

Fig. 11-3. A, Ankle strapping. Applying two stirrups. **B,** Ankle strapping for heel lock. **C,** Completed ankle strapping without heel lock.

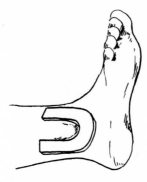

Fig. 11-4. Ankle horseshoe.

the instep and bringing it behind the ankle, hooking the heel, bringing it under the arch, up on the opposite side, and finishing at the starting point. The tape continues on the opposite side, hooking the heel, crossing the arch, and then returning to the starting point, completing two loops of the heel. The purpose of the heel lock is to stabilize the heel and the talus bone.

An additional technique that can be used by itself or in conjunction with the ankle strapping is application of an adhesive felt horseshoe (Fig. 11-4). The horseshoe technique also can be used in conjunction with the chronically swollen ankle and the tendons that might be strained in that area. Using ¼-inch adhesive felt, a horseshoe is cut to fit around the outer or medial malleolus.

The dancer should note that the use of elastic material in an attempt to support the ankle is discouraged. Yielding elastic material cannot adequately stabilize a joint. However, in situations in which there is swelling and the dancer desires to hold another bandage in place, an elastic wrap or tape may be useful.

A good test for the dancer to determine whether or not an ankle support should be worn is to jump up and down on the affected foot several times. An ankle that has recovered from an injury will usually allow the dancer to spring into the air and support the body on landing.

Knee sprain

The knee joint is made up of many individual joints with articulations between the two femoral condyles, between portions of the knee cartilage (menisci), between the tibia and the knee cartilage, and between the kneecap and thigh bone. All these individual articulations serve to make the knee one of the most complex joints in the human body (Fig. 11-5). In addition, the knee has a complex system of bursa sacs and a synovial membrane sheath that serves to lubricate the various anatomical structures. The knee cartilage is intended to

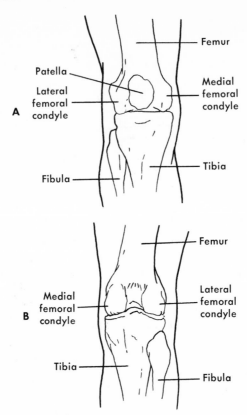

Fig. 11-5. Knee anatomy: **A,** front view; **B,** back view. Knee ligaments: **C,** front view; **D,** back view.

slightly deepen the joint and to cushion some of the stresses placed on the knee by leaping, running, and other vigorous locomotor activities common to dance. The menisci (knee cartilage) are held loosely on the tibia by ligaments around their outer border. When these ligaments are disrupted and torn, the knee cartilage becomes a loose body within the joint. Stabilizing the knee front to back and back to front are the cruciate ligaments. These ligaments function to prevent the femur from sliding back and forth when the leg is stabilized and, conversely, prevent the leg from sliding back and forth on the femur when it is fixed. Two ligaments provide the knee with side (lateral) stability and are known as the collateral knee ligaments. When the knee is completely straight, the cruciate and both collateral ligaments are tight. In a semiflexed position the cruciates loosen along with the lateral collateral ligaments so that the primary stabilizing element of the knee becomes the medial collateral ligament.

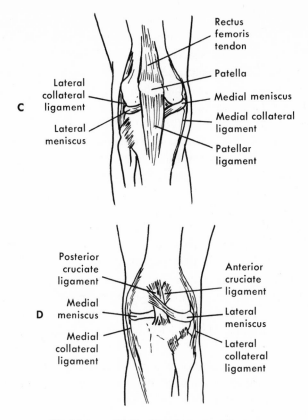

Fig. 11-5, cont'd. For legend see opposite page.

The sprained knee in dance occurs much less often than the strain; however, under adverse conditions the dancer can acquire a severely sprained knee. The primary cause of knee sprain in dance is from the sudden torsion, or twist, of the body with the affected leg planted or fixed to the floor. Under these circumstances both the collateral ligaments and the cruciates could be affected if the knee is slightly flexed. It is not typical for a single acute traumatic situation to cause a knee sprain. Repeated torsion injuries to the knee gradually cause a general laxity in all of the supporting ligaments, making the knee increasingly vulnerable to injury.

A controversial factor in the causation of knee injury is the deep knee bend. Some authorities say that the deep knee bend should be avoided at all costs because it tends to stretch the internal cruciate ligament, producing an unstable knee. This is particularly true when deep knee bends are initiated along with supporting heavy weight. I believe that full flexion of the knee is normal and can be initiated safely if performed under controlled conditions. Therefore the dancer is cautioned against sudden uncontrolled ballistic squats that tend to open up the knee joint suddenly, tearing its internal supporting ligaments. Also, pliés executed under controlled conditions with the thigh, leg, ankle, and foot maintained in good alignment do not normally injure the knee.

The teacher of dance should realize that different body builds coupled with a given set of situations can make the dancer more or less prone to knee injury. For example, a poorly conditioned dancer may not have the muscle control to prevent bouncing on the knees in a squat position; therefore, until conditioning is appropriate, grand pliés should be postponed. Also, the short-limbed, stocky, or heavily thigh muscled dancer may be more prone to knee injury than the long, lanky person because in the grand plié position the bulky thigh tends to bulge, causing the knee joint to be adversely forced opened.

The degree of knee sprain is often difficult to assess accurately. The best time to determine the extent of any injury is immediately after it occurs. The longer the period before assessment, the less accurate will be its determination. Because of the complexity of the knee, the extent of pathologic damage is often masked by rapid swelling. Making a completely accurate examination after 24 hours is almost impossible.

Evaluation is first made by observing the dancer's ability to support body weight on the affected leg. Often when the knee is seriously injured the dancer is unable to place the foot flat on the floor and is forced to walk on the toes of the injured leg. Observation may also reflect very rapid swelling in and about the knee joint. A second factor in determining the extent of a knee sprain is by palpating for tender areas. First, the soft musculature is felt and then the bone, capsular, and ligamentous tissue. If tenderness is elicited on palpation of capsular and ligamentous tissue, one might conclude that the knee support structures have been affected. The next factor in determining the seriousness of a knee sprain is to assess the extent of abnormal mobility present. This must be done before effusion (fluid accumulation) has occurred in the knee to mask the injury. Laxity in either of the collateral ligaments will be demonstrated by abnormal movement in a lateral or medial direction. Laxity in the cruciate ligament will display an anterior or posterior instability.

It is of the utmost importance that cold, compression by an elastic wrap, and elevation be applied immediately to the sprained knee. In addition to the general management procedures listed in Table 5, the dancer should engage in a program of immediate knee strength maintenance. The quadriceps muscles, the main extensor muscles of the knee, atrophy faster than almost any muscle in the body when not used. To prevent this problem, the dancer should immediately engage in a program of reconditioning. While the knee is being treated with cold, pressure, and elevation, the dancer should engage in muscle setting, which includes statically contracting and relaxing the quadriceps muscles with the knee kept in a fully extended position. Muscle setting maintains stimulation to the quadriceps muscle and helps to decrease atrophy. At no time, however, should the injured knee be flexed and extended in the initial acute stage; it should be kept in a fully extended position. After quadriceps setting, the dancer can progress into reconditioning exercises by executing straight leg raises from the front lying position and back lying position as well as brushes (tendu). The dancer must always remember not to bend the knee until the acute symptoms have been overcome. Following the acute stage the dancer can engage in a graduated program of knee flexion and extension, gradually regaining a full range of joint movement. Once range of movement exercises have begun, a program of progressive resistance exercises can begin with very light resistance at first.

The dancer is ready to return to full dance activity when the knee has redeveloped its strength and full range of movement and can withstand the stresses of lateral body movements without pain or instability.

Often a tape support is beneficial in the later stages of a knee sprain. Tape support is much preferred to elastic wraps and braces, which for the most part do not provide sufficient stabilization. Because the dancer needs complete knee mobility, it is extremely difficult to apply tape that will allow adequate movement and provide stabilization at the same time. Two techniques of strapping are presented; they can be added to or modified, depending on individual needs.

Technique A: X *knee strapping* (Fig. 11-6). This technique is designed to assist the dancer when there is lateral or medial instability. The tape is applied in a pattern executed for both sides of the knee. However, in a dance situation this may drastically restrict knee mobility, and therefore only the affected side should be taped. The primary materials needed are 2-inch linen tape, 3-inch elastic tape, and skin adherent. A circular 2-inch linen tape strip is placed as an anchor around the thigh approximately 8 to 10 inches above the patella and around the center of the calf. These anchor strips should be applied loosely; they can be very restricting as the muscle expands from being engorged with blood. An X pattern is applied to the area over the sprain. If both sides of the knee are to be taped, the X's would be initiated in an alternate pattern. Each X should start behind the medial condyle from the lower anchor strip and be carried

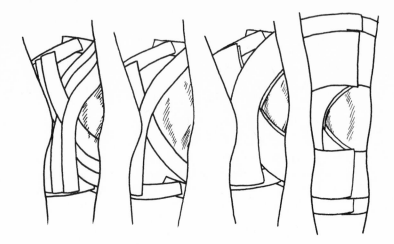

Fig. 11-6. X knee strapping.

upward, attaching to the thigh anchor strip. A series of three X's is applied. However, the dancer should be cautious not to restrict the kneecap, mainly because the patella must not be restricted if the knee is to bend. The X strips nearest the bend of the kneecap should be tucked under about ¼ inch along their outer border to protect the top from tear. Once the linen tape is in place a 3-inch elastic strip is applied over the X. The tape is locked in place by encircling the thigh and calf with elastic tape strips. If elastic tape is not available to the dancer, then an elastic wrap can be applied with a spiral technique over the linen tape to ensure that the tape does not loosen.

Technique B: rotary knee strapping (Fig. 11-7). Rotary knee strapping is designed for knee torsion injuries. Materials needed are 3-inch elastic tape, skin adherent, and a 4-inch pad. As in technique A, the knee is bent approximately 15 degrees. A 10-inch piece of elastic tape is cut and nipped at both ends and torn about 4 inches from its center. A gauze pad is placed behind the knee, and the 4-inch center of the torn elastic tape is placed directly over the gauze pad. The torn ends of the elastic tape strip are pulled taut, overlapping in front of the knee on either side of the patella. The second phase starts at the middle of the gastrocnemius with the application of a 3-inch elastic tape strip. The tape is brought to the front of the leg and then directly behind the knee, ending in front of the thigh. Only one strip should be applied in cases where the dancer requires a great deal of mobility. If a great deal of knee instability is present, the spiral strips can be retraced with additional strips of elastic tape. Once in place, the spirals are locked with elastic strips around both the thigh and calf.

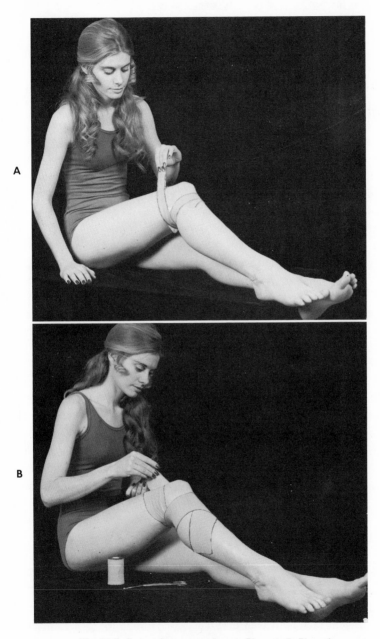

Fig. 11-7. Rotary knee strapping. **A,** Phase 1. **B,** Phase 2.

Hip sprain

Because the hip joint is the strongest and one of the best protected joints in the body, it seldom is sprained. However, even though the hip joint is well supported by bone, ligaments, and muscles, it can be sprained if it is put in a sudden abnormal position. Sprain of the hip joint most often occurs when the foot of the dancer is firmly planted on the floor and the trunk is suddenly forced into an awkward or opposing direction. The most obvious sign of a sprain is inability to move the thigh in a circular motion. A dancer who warms up properly and stretches the hip in all directions seldom receives a sprain. However, the dancer is most prone to chronic sprains of the hip in which the supporting capsule and ligaments are overstretched for a long period of time. Under these conditions, the capsule and ligaments become unable to maintain the head of the femur firmly in the hip socket and the dancer often complains of the hip feeling like it goes in and out of place when placed in a particular position.

The depth of the tissue surrounding the hip joint makes physical therapy difficult to administer. Rest of the injured hip joint gives the most positive reward. When symptoms of sprain have significantly subsided, a program of gradual stretching can be started. However, it is important that the hip region regain tone and strength of all the major muscles in that area. A strength program is necessary because ligamentous tissue once stretched can only be tightened by surgical intervention; therefore muscle strength must then replace these supporting structures.

Low back sprain

The low back injury was discussed at some length in Chapter 10; however, in this section the deeper injuries will be discussed. As in many body regions, it is often difficult to ascertain if an injury is muscular or involves the deeper joint structures or both. This is particularly true of the low back region. There are many terms that describe a low back condition, most of which are misleading or too general to really pinpoint the exact nature of a condition. These expressions are sciatica, lumbosacral sprains, and sacroiliac sprain.

Most injuries to the low back region are the result of repeated acute injuries, not just one episode of a sudden twist or extension movement. The structurally deformed or muscularly weak low back is highly susceptible to stress and pathologic damage.

A *radiating pain* down the leg when the back is moved can be caused by several different factors. A pain that radiates down the leg to the knee may be the result of pressure on the large sciatic nerve or impingement on nerves in the

Fig. 11-8. Low back exercise.

lumbar region. Dancers should be concerned and seek professional help if they have a backache with radiating pain, numbness, and/or a tingling sensation.

Repeated trauma to the low back can eventually result in a herniated disc. The tendency toward this problem can be increased by degeneration of a disc that has become narrow from repeated stresses and abnormal tensions in that area. A movement that suddenly increases the pressure of the internal viscous material (the nucleus pulposus) located in the center of the disc may force a rupturing and spilling of this material outside the vertebrae, placing painful pressure on spinal nerves. The gnawing and chronically painful low back may be caused by a herniated disc. A dancer with low back pain that fails to respond to normal physical therapy should be referred to a physician. The dancer should realize that the herniated disc often requires surgery. In almost every case low back sprain must be treated as a chronic problem that responds best to the conservative treatment of rest, sleeping on a firm surface or water bed, superficial and deep heat, and mild stretching. In cases of low back problems the strengthening of abdominal muscles and stretching of the low back must be considered in addition to realigning the pelvis if lordosis is present.

A good exercise for strengthening the low back is for the dancer to lie on his back on a flat surface with the knees bent up (Fig. 11-8). The dancer rolls the pelvis forward, flattening the low back. While holding this position, the pelvis is raised from the table 2 to 3 inches and held for a count of 10.

Dislocation (Table 6)

Dislocation is mentioned briefly here because it belongs in the category of the most severe of joint sprains. Although uncommon in dance, complete

Table 6. Chronic joint injury management*

Common conditions	Basic signs	Management phase	Treatment program			
			Physical therapy	Dosage	Reconditioning	Dosage
Recurrent dislocation, arthritis, and osteochondritis	Continuous low-grade inflammation in and around joint producing constant pain on movement, local weakness, and swelling	Symptomatic	1. Superficial heat	Three times daily	1. Rest of part	
			2. Analgesic balm	Three times daily	2. Movement of part to maintain range of movement	Three times daily
			3. Massage	Three times daily	3. General sustained exercise	Twice daily
			4. Deep heat	Three times daily		

*Adapted from Klafs, C. E., and Arnheim, D. D.: Modern principles of athletic training, ed. 3, St. Louis, 1973, The C. V. Mosby Co.

dislocation, or luxation, means that there is a complete disassociation of the body parts that make up a joint. More common, however, is partial dislocation, or subluxation, which is often described by the dancer as "I felt it go out and then it seemed to snap back in." In dance the serious toe stub can result in a dislocation; falling on the outstretched hand can cause the fingers to become dislocated.

However, the most common dislocation in dance, with the highest incidence among female dancers, is the kneecap that "goes out of place." Individuals with poor quadriceps muscle tone or those with a shallow recess for the patella to glide on seem to be susceptible to this problem. The increased angle of pull of the quadriceps tendon as a result of the wider hip has been suggested as the reason females have a higher incidence of patella dislocation than males. This problem, coupled with a congenital flattening of the lateral femoral condyle where the patella is recessed, increases the possibility of dislocating the kneecap. The right circumstance (such as having the patella knocked or hit by another dancer when the quadriceps is relaxed) can cause the patella to slide over and become lodged on the lateral aspect of the knee. For example, not turning the knee out and over the foot on the first step of a triplet turn (the plié) can force the kneecap to be pulled laterally. In this situation the dancer is unable to move the leg and is caught with the knee in a semiflexed position. It is obvious that this situation is a medical problem, but ice and pressure should still be applied to control the hemorrhage until a physician can give treatment. Following reduction of this dislocation, a cast or rigid bandage may be applied for 2 or 3 weeks.

It is also true that dancers complain that they feel their hip "go out" when they move in a particular way. This is particularly true for those who have overstretched the hip joint ligament and capsule. It is important that the dancer who has a loose hip problem avoid extreme stretching movements that cause the hip joint to be continually subluxated; this can eventually result in degeneration and a subsequent osteoarthritic problem. For dancers with chronically dislocating hips, it is suggested that they engage in a vigorous muscle conditioning program and avoid hip stretching until there is extremely good muscle tone and control in that area.

Joint degeneration (Table 6)

Sometimes occurring to the dancer's joints, particularly those of the hip and knee, is a degenerative condition that results in a softening of the articular surfaces. This degenerative condition seems to be more apparent in late childhood and young adolescence, but the results of this problem can be carried over into adulthood and even old age. Because of the softening of the articular surface, pieces of material are sloughed off into the joint, often getting caught during movement and making the so-called "creaking" noises. Loose bodies in a joint are commonly called "joint mice." This type of degeneration can react with pain, swelling, and other signs of a general inflammation. Teachers of dance should refer any student with these symptoms to a physician. The treatment of choice is often rest with decreasing amounts of weight bearing until nature has been allowed to resolve this problem.

Fractures

Although fractures that occur as a result of being hit are rare in dance, the fracture does occur as a result of a sudden twist or chronic stress. As mentioned earlier, fractures can be associated with a severe wrenching of a joint and a sudden pulling of muscle in which bone is pulled away. More commonly, fractures occur in dance because of chronic fatigue in a particular body part, causing agonist and antagonist muscles to pull at the same time, producing a shearing action on a particular bone. In this situation the spontaneous or stress fracture occurs. The most common sites for stress fractures in dancers are the metatarsal region of the foot and less commonly the fibula. The dancer should always be encouraged to refer to a physician any injury that fails to respond to first aid and palliative treatment.

Glossary

abduction. Movement of a part away from the midline of the body (opposite of adduction).

abrasion. Superficial wound of the skin resulting from friction or scraping the skin against a hard surface such as the floor.

acute. Sharp, abrupt, sudden, such as acute pain; there is a quick onset and the course is usually short in duration.

adduction. Movement of a part toward the midline of the body (opposite of abduction).

agonist muscle. The muscle or muscle group that is acting or contracting.

antagonist muscle. The muscle or muscle group that is in opposition to the agonist (contracting) muscle.

anterior. Situated in front of or in the forward part.

arm backward extension. Backward movement of the arm at the shoulder from a neutral starting position at the side of the body.

articulation. Place at which bones meet to form a joint.

avulsion. Tearing or pulling away of a part of a structure.

ballistic stretch. Bouncing stretch.

basketweave. Method of strapping by interweaving tape to provide extra strength.

bursa. Small closed sac that is lined by specialized connective tissue and contains synovial fluid; usually located over bony prominences where muscles or tendons glide.

cartilage. Specialized form of connective tissue with varying amounts of intercellular matrix that is nonvascular and found in various parts of the body.

charleyhorse. Contusion of quadriceps muscle characterized by pain and swelling produced by intramuscular bleeding.

chronic. Marked by long duration; continued; not acute; may also refer to a recurrent injury or one that has not responded to treatment.

contusion. Bruise of superficial or deep body tissues without a break in the covering of the skin; caused by external force.

167

counterirritant. Agent that is applied to the skin surface to produce a mild irritation and an analgesic effect.

dislocation. Either a partial or complete displacement of a bone from its normal position in a joint.

ecchymosis. Collection of blood under the skin (black and blue color)

epiphysis. That part of a bone that is concerned with growth in length (for example, the ends of the long bones).

eversion. Turning the sole of the foot outward, away from the midline of the body.

extension. Returning to a starting position in a hinge joint such as an elbow or knee; stretching a limb outward (opposite of flexion).

fascia. Fibrous membrane that covers, supports, and separates muscles.

flexion. Movement away from extension in a hinge joint such as the elbow and knee; a bending movement (opposite of extension).

fracture. Broken bone.

genu recurvatum. Hyperextension of the knee joint.

genu valgum. Knock-knee.

genu varum. Bowleg.

gradual stretch. Stretching musculotendinous unit by assuming a position in which the muscle is stretched gradually (opposite of ballistic stretch).

hamstring muscles. Muscles in the back of the thigh (biceps femoris, semitendinosus, and semimembranosus) that extend the thigh and flex the leg at the knee.

heel lock. Process of stabilizing the heel with tape or a wrap.

hematoma. Circumscribed collection of blood in a muscle following trauma.

hot spot. Hot or irritated feeling on the foot that occurs just before a friction blister occurs.

inflammation. Reaction of tissues to an injury or infection; characterized by heat, swelling, redness, pain, and sometimes loss of function.

inversion. Turning of the sole of the foot inward, toward the midline of the body.

isometric. Form of muscular contraction in which the muscle length does not change.

isotonic. Form of muscular contraction in which the length of the muscle changes.

laceration. Skin tear having jagged edges.

lateral. On the outer side, as distinguished from the medial (inner) side.

ligament. Band of fibrous connective tissue that stabilizes joints.

lumbosacral. Concerning the area of the back where the lumbar and sacral areas are in contact.

luxation. Complete dislocation.

medial. On the middle or inner side, as compared to the lateral (outer) side.

meniscus. Semilunar cartilage of the knee joint.

muscle stretch facilitation. Muscle relaxation through inhibition of antagonist muscle to increase a muscle stretch.

pinched nerve. Compression of a nerve root causing a contusion of the root.

plantar. Referring to the sole of the foot.

posterior. Behind or in back of.

reduction. Return to a normal position, as in reduction of a dislocated shoulder.

rubefacient. Substance that causes the skin to redden when applied topically.

scoliosis. Lateral curvature of the spine.

shin splints. Painful and disabling condition of the lower leg that results from a muscle strain.

spasm. Involuntary contraction of one or more muscles.

sprain. Injury of the supporting ligaments and other tissue associated with a joint following and as a result of a sudden twist.

static stretch. Gradual stretch.

strapping (taping). Use of adhesive tape to support or protect a joint.

subluxation. Partial or incomplete dislocation.

tendinitis. Irritation, inflammation, and swelling of a tendon.

tendon. Band of fibrous connective tissue that forms the end of a muscle and inserts into a bone controlling the direction of muscle pull.

tenosynovitis. Inflammation of the tendon sheath.

traumatic injury. Bodily injury caused by an external force.

wrapping. Use of cloth or elastic bandages to support or protect a joint.

Suggested readings

Arnheim, D. D., Auxter, D., and Crowe, W. C.: Principles and methods of adapted physical education, ed. 3, St. Louis, 1973, The C. V. Mosby Co.

Bogert, J., Briggs, G. M., and Calloway, D. H.: Nutrition and physical fitness, ed. 9, Philadelphia, 1973, W. B. Saunders Co.

Featherstone, D. F.: Dancing without danger, Cranbury, N. J., 1920, A. S. Barnes & Co., Inc.

Gelabert, R.: Anatomy for the dancer, New York, 1964, Dance Magazine.

Klafs, C. E., and Lyon, M. J.: The female athlete, St. Louis, 1973, The C. V. Mosby Co.

Klafs, C. E., and Arnheim, D. D.: Modern principles of athletic training, ed. 3, St. Louis, 1973, The C. V. Mosby Co.

Sparger, C.: Anatomy and ballet, ed. 3, London, 1960, Adam & Charles Block.

appendix

Suggested dance injury supplies

1. Elastic wrap, sizes 2, 3 or 4, and 6 inch; can be purchased in most drugstores and sporting goods stores.
2. Linen athletic tape, sizes ½, 1, 1½, and 2 inch–preferred tape for dancers is Johnson & Johnson porous coach-tape because it is lightweight and easily applied; can be purchased in sporting goods stores.
3. Elastic tape, sizes 2 or 3 inch–Johnson & Johnson Elastikon; can be purchased in sporting goods stores.
4. Spray tape adherent (clear); can be purchased in sporting goods stores.
5. Talcum powder; can be purchased in drugstores.
6. Lanolin; can be purchased in drugstores.
7. Dermassage medicated skin cream; can be purchased in drugstores.
8. Moleskin; can be purchased in drugstores.
9. Adhesive sponge rubber (Dr. Scholl's); can be purchased in drugstores.
10. Pretape wrap material; can be purchased in sporting goods stores.
11. Lamb's wool; can be purchased in drugstores.
12. Chemical cold pack; can be purchased in sporting goods stores.

Index